INTRODUC
ISSUES WI
OPPOSING
VIEWPOINTS

S0-AKH-821

Service, Emotional Support, and Therapy Animals

M. M. Eboch, Book Editor

GREENHAVEN
PUBLISHING

Published in 2022 by Greenhaven Publishing, LLC
353 3rd Avenue, Suite 255, New York, NY 10010

Articles in Greenhaven Publishing anthologies are often edited for length to meet page requirements. In addition, original titles of these works are changed to clearly present the main thesis and to explicitly indicate the author's opinion. Every effort is made to ensure that Greenhaven Publishing accurately reflects the original intent of the authors. Every effort has been made to trace the owners of the copyrighted material.

Library of Congress Cataloging-in-Publication Data

Names: Eboch, M. M., editor.
Title: Service, emotional support, and therapy animals / M. M. Eboch, book
  editor.
Description: First edition. | New York : Greenhaven Publishing, 2022. |
  Series: Introducing issues with opposing viewpoints | Includes
  bibliographical references and index. | Audience: Ages 12–15 | Audience:
Grades 7–9 | Summary: "The viewpoints in this volume explore the expanding world of assistance animals, shedding a light on how they do—and don't—enhance our lives"— Provided by publisher.
Identifiers: LCCN 2020050032 | ISBN 9781534507999 (library binding) | ISBN
  9781534507982 (paperback)
Subjects: LCSH: Service dogs—Juvenile literature. | Animals as aids for
  people with disabilities—Juvenile literature.
Classification: LCC HV1569.6 .S47 2022 | DDC 362.4/0483—dc23
LC record available at https://lccn.loc.gov/2020050032

Manufactured in the United States of America

Website: http://greenhavenpublishing.com

Contents

Foreword

Indulging in a wide spectrum of ideas, beliefs, and perspectives is a critical cornerstone of democracy. After all, it is often debates over differences of opinion, such as whether to legalize abortion, how to treat prisoners, or when to enact the death penalty, that shape our society and drive it forward. Such diversity of thought is frequently regarded as the hallmark of a healthy and civilized culture. As the Reverend Clifford Schutjer of the First Congregational Church in Mansfield, Ohio, declared in a 2001 sermon, "Surrounding oneself with only like-minded people, restricting what we listen to or read only to what we find agreeable is irresponsible. Refusing to entertain doubts once we make up our minds is a subtle but deadly form of arrogance." With this advice in mind, Introducing Issues with Opposing Viewpoints books aim to open readers' minds to the critically divergent views that comprise our world's most important debates.

Introducing Issues with Opposing Viewpoints simplifies for students the enormous and often overwhelming mass of material now available via print and electronic media. Collected in every volume is an array of opinions that captures the essence of a particular controversy or topic. Introducing Issues with Opposing Viewpoints books embody the spirit of nineteenth-century journalist Charles A. Dana's axiom: "Fight for your opinions, but do not believe that they contain the whole truth, or the only truth." Absorbing such contrasting opinions teaches students to analyze the strength of an argument and compare it to its opposition. From this process readers can inform and strengthen their own opinions, or be exposed to new information that will change their minds. Introducing Issues with Opposing Viewpoints is a mosaic of different voices. The authors are statesmen, pundits, academics, journalists, corporations, and ordinary people who have felt compelled to share their experiences and ideas in a public forum. Their words have been collected from newspapers, journals, books, speeches, interviews, and the internet, the fastest growing body of opinionated material in the world.

Introducing Issues with Opposing Viewpoints shares many of the well-known features of its critically acclaimed parent series, Opposing Viewpoints. The articles allow readers to absorb and compare divergent perspectives. Active reading questions preface each viewpoint, requiring the student to approach the material thoughtfully and carefully. Photographs, charts, and graphs supplement each article. A thorough introduction provides readers with crucial background on an issue. An annotated bibliography points the reader toward articles, books, and websites that contain additional information on the topic. An appendix of organizations to contact contains a wide variety of charities, nonprofit organizations, political groups, and private enterprises that each hold a position on the issue at hand. Finally, a comprehensive index allows readers to locate content quickly and efficiently.

Introducing Issues with Opposing Viewpoints is also significantly different from Opposing Viewpoints. As the series title implies, its presentation will help introduce students to the concept of opposing viewpoints and learn to use this material to aid in critical writing and debate. The series' four-color, accessible format makes the books attractive and inviting to readers of all levels. In addition, each viewpoint has been carefully edited to maximize a reader's understanding of the content. Short but thorough viewpoints capture the essence of an argument. A substantial, thought-provoking essay question placed at the end of each viewpoint asks the student to further investigate the issues raised in the viewpoint, compare and contrast two authors' arguments, or consider how one might go about forming an opinion on the topic at hand. Each viewpoint contains sidebars that include at-a-glance information and handy statistics. A Facts About section located in the back of the book further supplies students with relevant facts and figures.

Following in the tradition of the Opposing Viewpoints series, Greenhaven Publishing continues to provide readers with invaluable exposure to the controversial issues that shape our world. As John Stuart Mill once wrote: "The only way in which a human being can make some approach to knowing the whole of a subject is by hearing what can be said about it by persons of every variety of opinion and studying all modes in which it can be looked at by every character of mind. No wise man ever acquired his wisdom in any mode but this." It is to this principle that Introducing Issues with Opposing Viewpoints books are dedicated.

Introduction

"When they walk into a hospital, a nursing home or a school, everyone's eyes light up at the sight of a therapy dog. It doesn't matter if it is the patient being visited or the staff—everyone smiles."

—Olga Oksman, *"Paws for Thought: How Pet Therapy Is Gaining Traction,"* The Guardian

Humans have a long history of using other animals for both companionship and work. Dogs in particular have been bred for work and can be trained to do a variety of jobs, from pulling sleds to sniffing out bombs. It's no wonder, then, that they have also been tasked with pulling wheelchairs and predicting or responding to a seizure or diabetic crash.

It's not all about work, though. Anyone who has a pet knows the comfort they can bring. Cuddling a cat or playing with a dog is a great way to feel better after a long day. Pet ownership is often believed to be good for mental health.

Can animals actually help us be healthier? Although people use animals in a variety of ways to support human health, little research has been done to examine the effects of some of these practices. People often believe in the benefits of animals because interacting with an animal feels good, not because of scientific investigation.

Service animals are the most widely accepted when it comes to human use. Service animals are typically dogs, although miniature horses are also legally classed as service animals. No other animals are. Service animals have been trained to perform specific tasks to assist people with disabilities. According to the Americans with Disabilities Act (ADA), "Service animals are working animals, not pets. The work or task a dog has been trained to provide must be directly related to the person's disability."

Therapy animals, on the other hand, provide therapy to people other than their handlers. They may visit schools, hospitals, nursing homes, and disaster sites. In some cases, they help with learning, as in programs where children read to dogs. In other cases, they simply offer comfort to someone who has experienced trauma. Little research has been done on the effects of therapy animals, but many people with experience in these programs feel they are beneficial.

Both service animals and therapy animals receive extensive training. Service animals may be trained by the person with the disability or by experienced trainers who then pass along the animal, along with training on how the person and animal can work together. Therapy animals are often trained by their handlers, with support from experienced trainers. These animals are initially chosen for their calm temperaments. The training includes practicing proper behavior in public. Service animals learn to ignore distractions and only follow commands from their person. Therapy animals work with a variety of people in different locations, so their training includes learning proper behavior when interacting with everyone from children to the elderly. A well-trained service or therapy animal should never act out in public.

Few people argue against the use of service animals or therapy animals by people in need. Emotional support animals (ESAs) are more contentious. An ESA is a pet that helps someone with an emotional or mental disability by providing companionship and affection. Little research has been done on the effectiveness of emotional support animals. Some medical professionals feel ESAs do not help and may even be harmful if they are used in place of other treatment.

By law, an ESA must be prescribed to a patient by a licensed mental health professional, such as a therapist, psychologist, or psychiatrist. However, getting a letter identifying a pet as an ESA is fairly easy. Scam companies even offer ESA letters without a doctor's referral. Any animal can be claimed as an ESA, from a lizard to a goat to a peacock.

ESAs don't have the same rights as service animals, but they do offer certain extra advantages. Someone with an ESA should be able to keep their pet even in housing that normally does not allow pets. They are also allowed to travel with the pet in the cabin of an airplane and do not have to pay an extra fee for the pet.

Laws protecting service animals have hefty fines if a business owner wrongly refuses to admit one. Most business owners find it easier to admit the animal, even if they suspect it is not a true service animal. Problems arise when a poorly trained ESA or pet masquerading as an assistance animal misbehaves. On airlines, animals claimed as ESAs have urinated and defecated on seats and in the aisles, climbed on passengers, and even bitten them.

In addition, some people are afraid of dogs or have animal allergies. Should they be forced to give up their flight or else be exposed to an animal that might cause them harm?

The animal's own health is a complication as well. Not all animals have the temperament to calmly handle being in public or traveling on an airplane. Most people do not specifically train their ESA. Some veterinarians and animal rights supporters argue that it is better for the animal to be left at home.

Finally, people who falsely claim their animal as a service or support animal make business owners and the public suspicious about all assistance animals. A business owner who has had a negative experience with an animal masquerading as a service dog might refuse to allow someone with a real service dog to enter.

How should these issues be handled? Some argue for stricter laws controlling assistance animals. The government could offer official licensing and require all assistance animals to apply for legal certification. However, that would put the burden of proof on people with disabilities, making their lives even more challenging. Besides, someone who is willing to lie about their animal might simply buy fake documents anyway.

Maybe society should change to be more pet friendly, so people don't have to jump through hoops in order to bring along an animal that comforts them. But this would not solve the problem of allergies, animal phobias, or ensuring that animals are properly trained to behave in public.

Perhaps we should leave things as they are, accepting that some people will abuse the system. That might be the only way to ensure that people with disabilities receive the help they need without an undue burden.

A wide range of viewpoints come from disability advocates, veterinarians, businesses, and people who have benefited from assistance animals. They explore the current debates in *Opposing Viewpoints: Service, Emotional Support, and Therapy Animals*, shedding light on this ongoing contemporary issue.

Chapter 1

How Do Assistance Animals Help People?

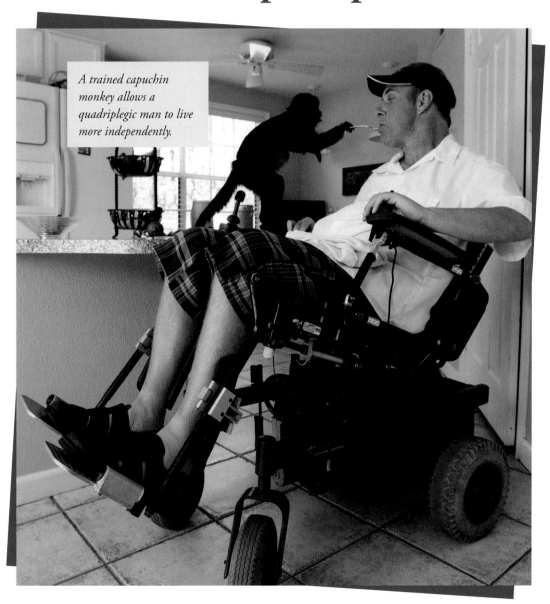

A trained capuchin monkey allows a quadriplegic man to live more independently.

Assistance Animals Can Help People in Different Ways

Lorraine Murray

"The sometimes uncanny natural abilities of animals can benefit humans in many ways."

In the following viewpoint, Lorraine Murray explores the history of humans using animals for assistance. Dogs and other animals can be trained to help people who are visually impaired or hearing impaired. They can also help people who use wheelchairs or have a variety of other special needs. Animals may also be trained as therapy animals. In this role, they help people make physical or mental improvements. Animals can also provide emotional support to people who are sad, lonely, or bored. Lorraine Murray is an editor and former manager of Advocacy for Animals.

AS YOU READ, CONSIDER THE FOLLOWING QUESTIONS:
1. How long have animals been used to help people with disabilities?
2. What animals are most commonly used as assistance animals?
3. How are assistance animals different from therapy animals?

The partnership between humans and animals dates back to the first domestication of animals in the Stone Age, as long as 9,000 years ago. But never have animals provided such dedicated and particular help to humans as they do today in the form of trained service, or assistance, to people with disabilities. These animals, usually dogs, help people accomplish tasks that would otherwise be prohibitively difficult or simply impossible. Service animals are not pets but working animals doing a job; thus, legislation such as the Americans with Disabilities Act (1990) in the United States and the Disability Discrimination Act (1995) in the United Kingdom makes service animals exempt from rules that prohibit animals from public places and businesses.

The most familiar service animals are guide dogs who help visually impaired people move about safely. Systematic training of guide dogs originated in Germany during World War I to aid blinded veterans. In the late 1920s Dorothy Harrison Eustis, an American dog trainer living in Switzerland, heard of the program and wrote a magazine article about it. The publicity led her to her first student, Morris Frank, with whose help she established a similar training school in the United States in 1929, the Seeing Eye (now located in New Jersey).

Guide-dog puppies are often bred for the purpose by the various organizations that train dogs. German shepherds, Labrador retrievers, and Labrador-golden retriever crosses are the most widely used breeds because of their calm temperaments, intelligence, natural desire to be helpful, and good constitutions. Puppies spend their first year with foster families who socialize them and prepare them for later training by teaching them basic obedience skills. At the age of approximately 18 months, guide dogs enter formal training, which lasts from about three to five months. During this period the dogs learn to adjust to a harness, stop at curbs, gauge the human partner's height when

Guide dogs undergo rigorous training, beginning with socialization at the puppy stage.

traveling in low or obstructed places, and disobey a command when obedience will endanger the person.

In recent years, hearing dogs have become increasingly common. These dogs, usually mixed-breed rescues from animal shelters, are trained to alert their human partners to ordinary sounds such as an alarm clock, a baby's cry, or a telephone. The dogs raise the alert by touching the partner with a paw and then leading him or her to the source of the sound. They are also trained to recognize danger signals such as fire alarms and sounds of intruders—again, by touching with a paw and then lying down in a special "alert" posture, at which time the human partner can take appropriate action.

Dogs can be trained for a great variety of assistance purposes. For example, Great Plains Assistance Dogs Foundation trains several categories of assistance animals, including service dogs, who help people who use wheelchairs and other mobility devices; hearing dogs; seizure-alert or -response dogs, who help persons with seizure disorders by activating an electronic alert system when symptoms occur (some can even predict the onset of a seizure); and therapeutic companion dogs, who provide emotional support for people in hospices, hospitals, and other situations in which loneliness and lack of stimulation are continual problems. There are many programs that train and certify pet animals, especially dogs and cats, as "therapy animals" who visit such institutions and bring much-welcomed companionship to patients.

Animals are also used in programs such as animal-assisted therapy (AAT). In the words of the Delta Society, AAT is a "goal-directed intervention" that utilizes the motivating and rewarding presence of animals, facilitated by trained human professionals, to help patients make cognitive and physical improvements. For example, an elderly patient in a nursing home might be given the task of buckling a dog's collar or feeding small treats to a cat, activities that enhance fine motor skills. Goals are set for the patients, and their progress is measured.

Dogs and cats are not the only animals who can assist humans with disabilities. Capuchin monkeys—small, quick, and intelligent—can help people who are paralyzed or have other severe impairments to their mobility, such as multiple sclerosis. These monkeys perform essential tasks such as turning on lights and picking up dropped objects. One of the more unusual assistance animals is the guide horse. An experimental program in the United States trains miniature horses to guide the visually impaired in the same way that guide dogs do. The tiny horses may be an alternative for people who are allergic to dogs or who have equestrian backgrounds and are more comfortable with horses.

Certain dogs and other animals have special skills similar to those of the seizure-assistance dogs, such as the ability to detect a diabetic's drop in blood sugar and alert the person before danger occurs. The sometimes uncanny natural abilities of animals can benefit humans in many ways. Reputable organizations that train assistance animals also take steps to ensure that the animals are cherished and lead rewarding, enjoyable, and healthy lives. When the animals' helping careers are over, provision is made for their well-deserved retirement.

EVALUATING THE AUTHOR'S ARGUMENTS:

Viewpoint author Lorraine Murray describes different ways animals can help people, ranging from guiding people with vision impairments to providing emotional support. Do you think all those things are equal? Should all support animals have the same rights in public? Why or why not?

There Are Rules for Businesses to Address Service Animals

"Distracting a working animal can be dangerous to the handler and the animal."

City of Portland

In the following viewpoint, the city of Portland, Oregon, explains some of the rules concerning service animals and other support animals. The piece is targeted at business owners who may be suspicious of people claiming to have service animals. Business owners are limited in the questions they can ask of someone with an animal. They cannot demand documentation. This viewpoint suggests business owners focus on addressing any specific problems an animal is causing, rather than worrying about whether the person with the animal is lying.

AS YOU READ, CONSIDER THE FOLLOWING QUESTIONS:
1. Why might someone with a service animal not have official documentation?
2. How could requiring documentation lead to discrimination?
3. Under what conditions could a business owner ask someone to take their service animal outside?

"March 2019: Animals, Animals Everywhere," City of Portland, Oregon, USA.

With serious, silly, and strange stories about service animals and emotional support animals making the news lately, it's no wonder there are lots of questions.

There is an abundance of resources on the many laws, etiquette questions, workplace wonderings, and common conundrums surrounding service and emotional support animals.

If you're looking for the CliffsNotes (or should I say Clifford's Notes?) read on!

What's the Difference Between Service Animals and Emotional Support Animals?

Service animals are trained to take a specific action to assist a person with a disability. Emotional support animals (sometimes called companion or comfort animals) provide disability-related emotional support.

A Bite-Sized Bit of Law

Service animals are protected under the rules for Titles II and III of the Americans with Disabilities Act (ADA). This means that service animals must be allowed any place the public is allowed, including restaurants, hotels, and hospitals.

Dogs, and in some cases miniature horses, are the only animals that can be recognized as service animals under the ADA. Under Oregon State Law, service-animals-in-training are also protected.

Emotional support animals are not specifically protected under the "in public" parts of the ADA, and they do not have to be allowed into public spaces.

And what about workplaces? Employers should fairly consider a request to bring a service or emotional support animal to the workplace like they would consider any other employee accommodation request.

The Fair Housing Act requires reasonable modifications to policy so that disabled people can use and enjoy our housing. It is common to modify a no-pet policy to allow service and emotional support animals. Any animal can be recognized as an emotional support animal.

A Doctor's Note

Both employers and landlords can ask for documentation from a health professional stating that an emotional support animal is required because of a disability.

If the need for a service animal is not obvious, employers and landlords can also ask for documentation from a health professional that a service animal is required because of a disability. This is different than in public places, where documentation cannot be requested.

Who Uses a Service Animal? And What Do Service Animals Do?

It is a common misconception that service animals are only used by people with visual disabilities.

Dogs can be trained to perform a variety of tasks like alerting their handlers to sounds, checking areas for a threat, detecting seizures, retrieving items, detecting low or high blood sugar, interrupting self-harm or distress, and more. As you might imagine, these services could be useful for people with many kinds of disabilities. And people may have different service dogs who are trained to do different things.

Service Animals Are NOT Leading the Way

Notice all those discrete and very specific tasks listed above? This is also an excellent opportunity to mention that service animals do not "guide" or "lead" blind people from place to place. Service dogs are responding to a series of commands given by their handlers. They are not canine GPS.

What About Emotional Support Animals?

Emotional support animals could be any kind of animal, and they are not usually specifically trained. Instead, their presence provides disability-related emotional support and alleviates symptoms of a disability, like lessening anxiety or depression.

What IF

To recap, service animals are highly trained to perform work or tasks to assist a person with a disability.

Not all service animals are providing an obvious service. This can put business owners in an uncomfortable situation.

Because service animals are allowed in any public place, there are still a lot of fears about badly-behaved service dogs disrupting business. Let's talk about some of the protections that exist and offer some brief thoughts on some of the most common "What IF's" out there.

What If I Think Someone Is Lying About Having a "Service Animal"?

Business owners and staff are allowed to ask two questions of anyone bringing in an animal they say is a service animal:

1. Is your dog required because of a disability?
2. What work or task is it trained to perform?

Questions about someone's disability, asking the dog to demonstrate the task, or requests for "certification" or other kinds of documentation are not allowed. Why? Well, disability is private, the task may not be demonstrate-able, and people are allowed to train their own service animal (meaning they may not have documentation).

This is a situation where we are balancing the right of people with disabilities to have some privacy and autonomy with the rights of business owners to protect their business and customers.

Registration and Certification: The Controversy Continues

With the increasing visibility of service animals, confusion over emotional support animals, and conversation around fraud, there are lots of people wondering why service animal handlers don't have to provide proof that their animal has been trained or registered as a service animal.

Properly training a service animal yourself is a long, arduous process. And yet getting a professionally trained animal from an organization means long waits and a high cost, including weeks or months of travel. Self-training with the assistance of a local trainer may be the only option. And this means no documentation or "official" certification.

The Cost of "Show Me Proof"

Requiring registration would also mean additional costs for both individuals and society, including financial, transportation, and administrative costs. And fraud could still be an issue.

And service animal handlers could potentially be stopped at every public place.

Would You Want to Show Paperwork Every Time You Went into a Business?

What if the paperwork itself were questioned? Or you forgot it? Or they didn't ask but you knew that they could at any time?

Besides being an ordeal just to run errands, history and current events shows us these kinds of rules are enforced in biased and harmful ways.

Racism, classism, ethnocentrism, heterosexism, transphobia, Islamaphobia, and other forms of oppression would likely affect when and how documentation rules would be enforced.

Requiring some form of registration or certification brings its own set of complex issues and is not a straightforward solution.

But Really, What If They're Lying?!

But I still think they're lying! That's why I asked those questions! What if they just lie?! [I can hear you vehemently exclaiming.]

Yes, it is awful to feel lied to. Some states agree and are trying to help.

And yet a more useful question to ask is: Why is this animal presenting a problem in this situation? Read on!

What If a Service Animal Is Bothering My Customers or Guests?

How is it "bothering" them? Is it barking, going up to people, making a mess on the floor, or being aggressive with people or other animals? This should generally not happen with a trained service animal, but if it does: You can ask that the handler control the service animal, and if that's not possible, to take it outside.

The individual should then be given the opportunity to come back without the animal.

What If a Service Animal Damages Property?

While people cannot be charged extra fees just for having a service animal in public (or an emotional support animal in their apartment), business owners and landlords can charge for any damage caused by an animal.

Just like a person is held liable for damage they (or their children or pets) cause at some businesses, service animal handlers are responsible for the damage their animals cause. Again, this should generally not happen with a trained service animal, but if it does, there are protections.

Bottom line? Any animal that is not behaving can be asked to leave.

What If People Are Allergic or Afraid of Dogs?

This is one of those situations that calls for creativity and working together. Can a service-animal user and person with allergies or fears be seated far away from each other? Can they agree to access the space at different times? What would it take to make this work? These ideas for the workplace might be a helpful place to start.

Rules of Engagement

Let's say someone isn't afraid of dogs or the damage they might cause. They love dogs! All dogs! And all animals! And they want to pet them! And talk about them! All. The. Time.

We hear you. We're with you. And if you have a free hour sometime, ask me about my cat.

The essence of staying cool:

1. Ask people if it's okay to pet their service animal.
2. Be okay if they say no. The animal is working, and distracting a working animal can be dangerous to the handler and the animal.
3. Think of other things to talk about with service animal handlers besides their animal. It's a new topic for you. It's perhaps a daily or hourly topic for a handler.

EVALUATING THE AUTHOR'S ARGUMENTS:

This viewpoint explains laws about service animals, including why official documentation is not required. Do the rules make sense to you? Why or why not? What are advantages and disadvantages to requiring people with service animals to provide documentation supporting the animal's role?

Animals Comfort Us

Olga Oksman

In the following viewpoint, Olga Oksman explores animal assisted therapy. A number of such animal assisted therapy programs exist. Some encourage children to read to dogs. Others help people with physical therapy. At disaster sites, animals may help people process emotions. While there are not yet set standards, typically therapy animals require weeks of training with their handlers. The use of therapy animals is relatively new, but it is growing. Olga Oksman is a journalist whose work has appeared in the *Financial Times*, *Guardian*, and *Forbes*.

"Petting a dog for a few minutes can raise levels of hormones that make us feel better."

AS YOU READ, CONSIDER THE FOLLOWING QUESTIONS:
1. Is there evidence that therapy helps people?
2. What qualities do therapy animals need?
3. Do therapy animals work better for certain types of people?

"Paws for Thought: How Pet Therapy Is Gaining Traction," by Olga Oksman, Guardian News & Media Limited, December 30, 2015. Reprinted by permission.

The volunteers all describe it the same way. When they walk into a hospital, a nursing home or a school, everyone's eyes light up at the sight of a therapy dog. It doesn't matter if it is the patient being visited or the staff—everyone smiles.

Animal assisted therapy, once rare and met with opposition as something unproven that would only bring germs into hospitals, is gaining traction. Many hospitals and nursing homes now have animal therapy programs in place, including at the Mayo Clinic, despite little evidence into the impact on patients in the long term.

"In the area of therapy animals, practice is far outpacing research. People think it works and like the idea of it, so they do it," explains Maggie O'Haire, assistant professor of human-animal interaction at Purdue University College of Veterinary Medicine.

One challenge as the practice has become more widespread has been explaining how exactly it works. "Positive changes from animal-assisted intervention are varied and there is no single pathway that has yet been identified," says O'Haire.

There are a number of theories as to why it works, however.

"One is the biophilia hypothesis—essentially that humans have an innate propensity to connect with other living things," says Sandra Barker, professor of psychiatry at Virginia Commonwealth University and director of the Center for Human-Animal Interaction at the university. Another is the social support theory—the idea that therapy animals provide a form of nonjudgmental support.

In the past ten years, animal assisted therapy, mostly conducted by nonprofit organizations staffed by volunteers, has expanded far beyond a visit to the surgery recovery room and cancer treatment center. Today, programs exist that provide animals who assist with physical therapy, help tutor children in reading and provide comfort in settings as disparate as disaster zones and university campuses.

While research on the subject still has a long way to go, the idea that animals are good for our health has been around for some time. There are cases of doctors trying to incorporate animals into psychiatric settings as far back as the 1700s, to try to calm patients and improve their quality of life. More recently, studies have shown that having a pet around can lower blood pressure, and the American

Therapy dogs can bring comfort to hospitalized patients, aiding in their recovery.

Heart Association has stated that owning a dog may even lower the risk of heart disease.

Dogs don't just make us calmer, some studies have shown that they also make us happier. Research has shown that just petting a dog for a few minutes can raise levels of hormones that make us feel better.

Nancy George-Michalson is the director of programs and education at New York Therapy Animals, an organization that sends animals and their human volunteers into hospitals, schools and other settings.

New York Therapy Animals is part of a program called Reading Education Assistance Dogs. Instead of having a child who may be struggling with reading to try to sound out words for a human tutor, the children read stories to a visiting dog, who sits patiently and listens, George-Michalson explains. The kids get so excited by the idea of reading to a dog that they often practice reading their chosen book before the dog's arrival so they can do a better job, says Bridgette McElroy, a teacher whose East Harlem school participates in the program.

The dog never gets frustrated if a child struggles to sound something out. No matter how slowly and with how much stumbling the story is read, the dog is happy to be there, providing both motivation for reading and a nonjudgmental listener.

Anecdotal evidence like this in support of animal therapy is constantly growing. George-Michalson remembers a particular resident at a nursing home where she and her peach-colored toy poodle, Callie, volunteered. The nursing home resident was a 99-year-old woman who did not have many visitors. Every week before George-Michalson and her dog arrived, the woman would ask for her walker and have someone help her down to the lobby so she could see Callie twirl and dance on the lobby carpet when they entered. Not only did the visits cheer the woman up, but seeing Callie's twirling motivated her to keep up her mobility by walking down to the lobby each week.

Getting patients to move is a common theme with therapy animals. Sitting in a sterile hospital room, going through the same motions every day with a physical therapist can be unmotivating. Rachel McPherson, founder and president of the Good Dog Foundation, remembers a particular patient at a hospital where she and her Pomeranian, Fidel, volunteered. The man was recovering from a stroke and needed to regain mobility in his hands. So Fidel would jump into his lap with a ball. The man would try to take the ball and throw it for Fidel to chase after.

At first Fidel had to put the ball into his hand, and it would drop to the floor as he could not grasp it firmly enough, but Fidel never minded. He would jump off the bed, pick up the ball and happily bring it right back to the man in his bed. Week after week, the man and Fidel would play their game until the man regained enough mobility in his hand and shoulder to hold the ball and pet and brush Fidel.

Animal assisted therapy has also been gaining traction at disaster sites. The Good Dog Foundation sent volunteers out during 9/11 and Katrina as well as the Boston Marathon bombing. When something so horrific occurs, people often are unable to immediately process it and speak to a therapist, explains McPherson. At that initial moment of trauma, a lick on the cheek is the most people can handle, she explains. New York Therapy Animals sent volunteers to help Fema staff cope during hurricane Sandy. George-Michalson vividly recalls how one of the Fema workers put his arms around a Golden Retriever and started sobbing into its fur. "The dogs offer this unconditional love, and seeing a man bending over a dog and sobbing is extraordinary" she says.

The stories can sometimes be truly heartbreaking. Barker remembers a mother whose daughter had died thanking her for bringing a therapy dog to visit the child before she passed away. That visit from the therapy dog was the last time the mother had seen her child smile, and it brought her some measure of comfort to have seen her daughter happy during her last moments.

Despite the stories and long history of the human bond with companion animals, it was only recently that hospitals started to allow therapy animals on their floors. When McPherson started the

Good Dog Foundation 18 years ago, it was still illegal in New York to bring an animal into a hospital, and she worked hard to help change that law. Now most hospitals in New York City allow therapy animals. Some hospitals have even started to allow patients to bring their own pets from home for a visit.

McPherson hopes that the increase in interest in animal assisted therapy will bring with it some standardization to the many programs that now exist. The Good Dog Foundation is consulting with the NIH to try to create standards for animal therapy that can be applied across volunteer organizations. Standardization of training is one step in a process that she hopes will end with insurance reimbursement for animal assisted therapy, allowing it to become even more commonplace.

Even without standardization and despite variability in training, the requirements to become a therapy dog are steep. While any breed or mutt can be a therapy dog, a certain kind of personality is required. "Visiting unfamiliar people in unfamiliar settings requires a well-trained, healthy dog, with a positive temperament and good manners," says Barker.

After a dog is chosen based on its easy personality and good behavior, it must go through an extensive training program to be a therapy dog and pass a test. The dog has to not just be trained to always follow commands, but to also learn things like how to walk around medical equipment at a hospital so it can be safe in any setting. At New York Therapy Animals, dogs and their handlers go through a six-week program. At the Good Dog Foundation, the dogs and handlers go through 11 classes before they graduate.

While dogs will never replace therapists and teachers, O'Haire hopes to see animal assisted therapy as an increasingly common compliment to existing mental health practices. The benefit from animal assisted therapy seems to be the same regardless of the person's background. Barker has found in her research that there is no difference in benefit from animal assisted therapy for people who do or don't own pets, and that the impact is universal, whatever someone's race or background.

As it turns out, a cold wet nose and a fuzzy face make just about all of us smile. Or, as an interpreter at the 9/11 site told McPherson when she was volunteering there with Fidel: "I don't need to be here with the dog, because the dog is complete love, and that is international."

The Science Doesn't Support Emotional Support Animals

Judith Tutin

"Why try therapy for your anxiety when you can just drag your pet around with you and talk to it?"

In the following viewpoint, Judith Tutin argues against the use of emotional support animals. She notes that the effectiveness of emotional support animals has not been studied in depth. While spending time with animals might make people happier, that's not the same as treating anxiety or depression. Other methods have been better tested and may be more effective. Some people asking for emotional support animals may be looking for a quick fix, while others may simply want permission to keep a pet with them. Judith Tutin is a psychologist and certified life coach.

"Why Your Emotional Support Animal Is NOT Treatment for Your Anxiety," by Judith Tutin, Tango Media Corporation, January 6, 2017. Reprinted by permission.

AS YOU READ, CONSIDER THE FOLLOWING QUESTIONS:

1. Are pet owners happier and mentally healthier than non-pet owners, in general?
2. Has it been proven that having a pet will reduce anxiety or depression?
3. How should people treat anxiety, according to the author?

I was on a recent teletherapy call with an anxious young college student. Let's call him Robbie. Halfway in he told me he thought he needed an ESA.

"ESA?" I thought. "Is that one of those texting anagrams I should know, like FOMO or YOLO?"

Before I had a chance to ask, Robbie said that having his long-time companion, his adored tabby, in his dorm room would make his anxiety manageable.

It came to me in a flash: Emotional Support Animal. I'd read about these.

A quick Google search after the call revealed that people are contacting teletherapy services, like the one I took Robbie's call on, to obtain virtually (pun intended) immediate certification to have their ESAs in dorms, pet-unfriendly apartments, and on airplanes.

Happily, I'd punted and suggested that, since he said the college counseling office at his school was "certifying" people to have ESAs, he ought to contact them if he thought it would be helpful.

I say happily because I didn't know step-one about what makes a pet certification-eligible. I never heard from him again which told me that his stated intention for teletherapy, to reduce his anxiety, was merely a ploy to get said certification.

I was relieved to be off the hook even before I read a recent scholarly article cautioning psychologists about providing such certifications.

The piece revealed that we assume being in the presence of animals has a therapeutic effect on people, "an assumption that does not appear to have substantial foundation in science."

The media was also blamed for incorrectly leading people "to believe that ESAs are effective for mitigating mental health problems."

Certain chicken breeds make them ideal, if unconventional, therapy animals. But their usefulness may only go so far.

Witness this headline that recently caught my eye, "How therapy chickens are helping people with anxiety." Really?

Just to be perfectly clear, I am NOT talking about Service Animals, regulated by the Federal government, which are animals (not pets) individually trained to perform tasks for disabled people.

Let me also clarify that there is a difference between the benefits of having a pet, and saying that a pet has a therapeutic effect on a psychiatric disorder like anxiety.

Pet owners, in one series of studies, were found to be healthier on a number of psychological dimensions and measures of well-being, like self-esteem, and they were less lonely and introverted.

But this does not mean that having a pet will significantly reduce serious anxiety or depression.

That same series of studies revealed that 25 percent of married or cohabitating pet-owners say their pet is "a better listener than their spouse." This concerns me, as does the comment I read in one article about ESAs: "Do I have to go to therapy to get a paper to keep an ESA?"

In other words, why talk to your spouse about problems or try therapy for your anxiety when you can just drag your pet around with you and talk to it?

Don't get me wrong, I love my kitties. They bring me joy, comfort and provide me with great company. I also love my partner, but I think he's a much better listener than either of my cats.

Notwithstanding the recent study finding that dogs understand language, I know my partner is a better listener because he's human. Not only does he comprehend everything I'm saying, he can respond in kind.

I also love my clients, some of whom have pets. But I don't think any find their pet a substitute for psychotherapy.

As I explained to Robbie, there were a number of things he might try to do to reduce his anxiety. Each of my suggestions was much more likely to significantly impact his anxiety than dragging his tabby to his dorm.

Instead of trying to find a mental health professional to confirm your need for an ESA, or paying one of those registries to certify your pet, put your energy to better use with effective strategies like these:

- Anxiety reduction (breathing, questioning problematic thoughts, positive self-talk).
- Stress reduction (meditation, music, getting in motion, gratitude).
- The relaxation response attained through a series of steps to relax the body and mind.
- Holding yourself accountable for using breathing, stress reduction or relaxation techniques regularly.
- Identifying issues in your life that might be contributing to your anxiety and spending time figuring out how to address said issues.

- Taking a hard look at your diet, sleep and exercise and working on needed adjustments.
- Considering whether you need a psychotherapist to assist you in customizing techniques that work for you and holding you accountable for practicing those techniques.
- Considering whether medication is appropriate to help you reduce anxiety.

I hate the fact that Robbie probably left our teletherapy session feeling like he didn't get what he needed. But I hope I planted the seeds that relaxation, exercise, sleep, a good diet and some time management skills might be more helpful to him at school, in the long run, than his beloved tabby.

EVALUATING THE AUTHOR'S ARGUMENTS:

Viewpoint author Judith Tutin contends that pets are less effective at treating anxiety and depression than other methods. Do you agree? Does the author's background as a clinical psychologist suggest expertise in the area, or bias, or both?

Therapy Dogs Provide Many Benefits

Christine Grové and Linda Henderson

"Research has shown therapy dogs can reduce stress and provide a sense of connection in difficult situations."

In the following viewpoint, Christine Grové and Linda Henderson argue in support of the use of therapy dogs. Therapy dogs are not trained service dogs. However, they and their owners are trained to interact with people safely. Working with therapy dogs can motivate people to learn and help them deal with traumatic situations. Visits with therapy animals leave people feeling happier and less stressed. Christine Grové is an educational and developmental psychologist. Linda Henderson teaches in the education department at Monash University in Australia and has studied therapy dogs.

AS YOU READ, CONSIDER THE FOLLOWING QUESTIONS:
1. What can happen psychologically for people using therapy dogs?
2. How can therapy dogs help children learn?
3. What perceived risks keep some schools from using therapy animals?

"Therapy Dogs Can Help Reduce Student Stress, Anxiety, and Improve School Attendance," by Christine Grové and Linda Henderson, The Conversation, March 19, 2018. https://theconversation.com/therapy-dogs -can-help-reduce-student-stress-anxiety-and-improve-school-attendance-93073. Licensed under CC-BY ND 4.0.

In the wake of the school shootings in Florida, therapy dogs have been used as a way to provide comfort and support for students returning to school. Research has shown therapy dogs can reduce stress and provide a sense of connection in difficult situations.

Given the impact therapy dogs can have on student well-being, schools and universities are increasingly adopting therapy dog programs as an inexpensive way of providing social and emotional support for students.

What Are Therapy Dogs?

It's important to note therapy dogs are not service dogs. A service dog is an assistance dog that focuses on its owner to the exclusion of all else. Service dogs are trained to provide specific support for individuals with disabilities such as visual or hearing difficulties, seizure disorders, mobility challenges, and/or diabetes.

The role of therapy dogs is to react and respond to people and their environment, under the guidance and direction of their owner. For example, an individual might be encouraged to gently pat or talk to a dog to teach sensitive touch and help them be calm.

Therapy dogs can also be used as part of animal assisted therapy. This aims to improve a person's social, cognitive and emotional functioning. A health care professional who uses a therapy dog in treatment may be viewed as less threatening, potentially increasing the connection between the client and professional.

FAST FACT

Therapy dogs may visit schools, day cares, nursing homes, hospitals, etc. They must have friendly, easygoing personalities because they interact with a variety of people.

There are also animal-assisted activities, which is an umbrella term covering many different ways animals can be used to help humans. One example is to facilitate emotional or physical mental health and wellbeing through pet therapy or the presence of therapy dogs. These activities aren't necessarily overseen by a professional, nor are they specific psychological interventions.

Therapy dogs are used in schools to support children who are learning to read.

Research suggests using therapy dogs in response to traumatic events can help reduce symptoms of depression, post traumatic stress disorder and anxiety.

So, what can happen psychologically for people using therapy dogs?

The Human-Animal Bond

The human-animal bond can impact people and animals in positive ways. Research shows therapy dogs can reduce stress physiologically (cortisol levels) and increase attachment responses that trigger oxytocin—a hormone that increases trust in humans.

Dogs also react positively to animal-assisted activities. In response to the human-animal bond, dogs produce oxytocin and decrease their cortisol levels when connecting with their owner. Often dogs feel the same when engaging in animal assisted activities as if they were at home, depending on the environmental context.

Benefits of Therapy Dogs
Animal assisted therapy can:
- teach empathy and appropriate interpersonal skills
- help individuals develop social skills
- be soothing and the presence of animals can more quickly build rapport between the professional and client, and
- improve individual's skills to pick up social cues imperative to human relationships. Professionals can process that information and use it to help clients see how their behaviour affects others.

More recently, therapy dogs are being used as a form of engagement with students at school and university.

Benefits of Therapy Dogs at School
A recent report highlighted children working with therapy dogs experienced increased motivation for learning, resulting in improved outcomes.

Therapy dogs are being used to support children with social and emotional learning needs, which in turn can assist with literacy development.

Research into the effects of therapy dogs in schools is showing a range of benefits including:
- increase in school attendance
- gains in confidence
- decreases in learner anxiety behaviours resulting in improved learning outcomes, such as increases in reading and writing levels
- positive changes towards learning and improved motivation, and
- enhanced relationships with peers and teachers due to experiencing trust and unconditional love from a therapy dog. This in turn helps students learn how to express their feelings and enter into more trusting relationships.

Despite these known benefits, many schools choose not to have therapy dog programs due to perceived risks. These range from concerns about sanitation issues to the suitability of dog temperament when working with children. But therapy dogs and owners are carefully selected and put through a strict testing regime prior to acceptance into any program.

The main reason for the lack of take up has been linked to the limited research into the benefits of therapy dogs in schools.

Benefits of Therapy Dogs at University

Researchers have found university students reported significantly less stress and anxiety, and increased happiness and energy, immediately following spending time in a drop-in session with a dog present, when compared to a control group of students who didn't spend any time with a therapy dog.

EVALUATING THE AUTHORS' ARGUMENTS:

Viewpoint authors Christine Grové and Linda Henderson list many benefits of using therapy dogs in educational settings. Compare this viewpoint to the previous one. Do they support or contradict each other? How so? Be sure to note the type of animal being discussed in each viewpoint.

Chapter 2

What Rights and Regulations Affect Assistance Animals?

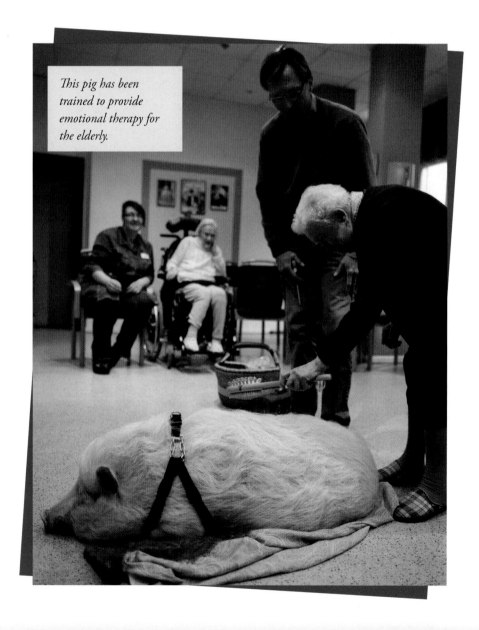

This pig has been trained to provide emotional therapy for the elderly.

It's Easy to Make a Pet an ESA

EZCare Medical Clinic

"You may be surprised at how easy it is to get a valid ESA letter."

In the following viewpoint, EZCare Medical Clinic explains the process of obtaining a letter that identifies a pet as an emotional support animal (ESA). The author calls the process easy but notes that scam companies offer ESA letters without a doctor's referral. According to the viewpoint, a legitimate letter requires consultation with a licensed medical professional, either in person or by video chat. EZCare Medical Clinic is a facility in San Francisco that offers online medicine, walk-in appointments, and ESA letters.

AS YOU READ, CONSIDER THE FOLLOWING QUESTIONS:
1. What conditions might allow someone to get an ESA?
2. Do you have to be receiving other treatment for the condition in order to get an ESA?
3. What types of animals can qualify as an ESA?

"How Difficult Is It to Get an ESA Letter?" EZCare Medical Clinic. Reprinted by permission.

I f you have an emotional or mental condition, you may already realize that the presence of a cherished pet can have a therapeutic effect. Many healthcare providers also recognize this fact, which is why it is now possible to get a letter to designate your pet as an emotional support animal. If you possess a legitimate ESA letter, your pet will be able to travel with you on airlines in the cabin with no added fees and they will also be able to live with you in housing that may not otherwise accept pets.

Though ESAs are not specially trained like Service Animals and therefore do not experience all the same benefits, they can still be highly valuable in your treatment plan. It's worth looking into getting an ESA letter for them so you can benefit from the laws that protect the animals and their owners. Though it may seem daunting at first to qualify for an ESA letter, the process is actually quite simple and you may be surprised at how easy it is to get a valid ESA letter.

Mental and Emotional Conditions That Qualify for ESA

Almost any emotional or mental issue can qualify you for an ESA if it is having a profound negative impact on your everyday life. Conditions such as anxiety, depression, post-traumatic stress syndrome, bipolar disorder, social anxiety, phobias, or similar conditions that can be helped by the presence of a pet all can qualify for an ESA. Most people who ask their doctors for an ESA letter already have a pet they consider therapeutic. However, some others acquire such a pet after they realize the many benefits of ESAs. Any type of animal can qualify as an ESA prescription, though the most common types of animals are cats and dogs due to how easy it is to travel with and care for them as well as their natural supportive natures.

FAST FACT

People request ESAs for many conditions, including anxiety, depression, post-traumatic stress syndrome, bipolar disorder, social anxiety, and phobias.

ESA Letter Process

It is not difficult to qualify for an ESA letter. If you are not currently seeing an LMHP [licensed mental health

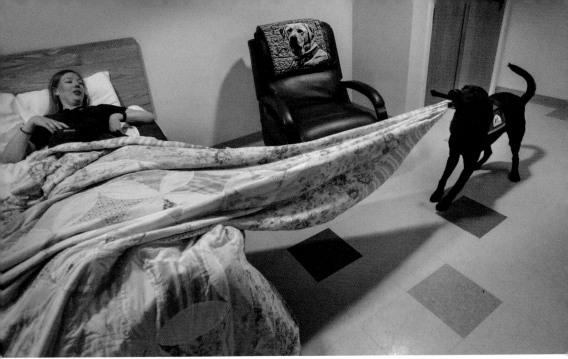
Soldiers suffering from PTSD can benefit from specially trained dogs that react to people having nightmares.

professional], you can still qualify for an ESA letter either in-person or online. You will speak to a licensed doctor via secure video chat or in-person, who will determine what condition you suffer from and if it would be helped by an ESA. If the therapist decides you are a good candidate for an ESA, he or she will issue a legitimate emotional support animal letter.

How to Spot an ESA Letter Scam
Unfortunately, there are many companies online that say they offer legitimate ESA letters but are actually scams. If the company says they will "register" your pet as an ESA or if they promise quick or cheap ESA letters, they are likely a scam. There is no need to register pets as ESA and, in fact, there are no recognized ESA registries in the country. Also, you can not get a legitimate ESA letter without speaking to a doctor. The doctor should speak to you in-person or online. Automatically approved letters are a SCAM! Legitimate ESA letters take the time and effort of an LMHP and therefore are not cheap or quick to obtain.

At EzCare Clinic, you will speak to a licensed doctor and receive a digital copy in 30–60 min after your consultation, and a hard copy in 3–5 business days via mail. A fake ESA letter can easily get you into trouble with your landlord or cause problems with your travel plans and should be avoided at all cost.

How to Choose the Right ESA Prescription Service

When you are looking for an emotional support animal prescription, it's crucial that you look for a service that has a physical clinic location where the LMHP works. If you choose EZ Care Medical Clinic, you will see that we have a money-back guarantee, have a physical location and verified LMHPs on staff, and our letters are valid in all states. You can apply at our clinic online or in person and we have doctors available seven days a week. We know how important it is for you to have a legitimate ESA letter so you can keep your cherished pet with you at all times. Our knowledgeable and professional staff will ensure that you get your letter as quickly as possible and that it will be accepted by all landlords and airlines.

If you have mental or emotional disorders such as anxiety, depression, social anxiety, or post-traumatic stress disorder and believe that an emotional support animal can help with your therapy, talk to your doctor about an ESA letter today. If you aren't currently seeing a doctor, choose a reputable online service such as the one offered at EZ Care Clinic so you can get a legitimate ESA prescription letter for your pet.

EVALUATING THE AUTHOR'S ARGUMENTS:

This viewpoint is written by a clinic that offers ESA letters. Does this source make you more or less likely to trust its advice? Why? If there are no recognized ESA registries in the country, what makes an ESA letter "legitimate"?

An Emotional Support Animal Is Not a Service Animal

"Emotional Support Animals do not have the formal training and tested temperament to move so freely in society."

Massachusetts Society for the Prevention of Cruelty to Animals–Angell

In the following viewpoint, Massachusetts Society for the Prevention of Cruelty to Animals–Angell argues that people might have trouble exercising their rights, depending on whether an animal is a service animal or an emotional support animal. The rules for service animals are covered under the Americans with Disabilities Act (ADA). ESAs have some rights in housing and on airplanes. These rights do not extend to restaurants and other businesses. Massachusetts Society for the Prevention of Cruelty to Animals–Angell Animal Medical Center is a nonprofit organization that protects animals.

AS YOU READ, CONSIDER THE FOLLOWING QUESTIONS:
1. How does the ADA relate to service animals?
2. What questions are business owners allowed to ask of people with support animals?
3. Why is it harder to gain access to businesses with a cat, rabbit, or guinea pig?

The MSPCA receives many phone calls from people who are denied access to public spaces with or have questions about their assistance animals. The information below should help you understand where you can bring or live with your assistance animal in Massachusetts.

What Kind of Assistance Animal Do You Have?

An important distinction to understand is that there are two broad groups of assistance animals:

Service Animals are defined as dogs* that are individually trained to do work or perform tasks for people with disabilities. Examples of such work or tasks include guiding people who are blind, alerting people who are deaf, pulling a wheelchair, alerting and protecting a person who is having a seizure, reminding a person with mental illness to take prescribed medications, calming a person with Post Traumatic Stress Disorder (PTSD) during an anxiety attack, or performing other duties. Service Animals are working animals, not pets. The work or task a dog has been trained to provide must be directly related to the person's disability. Dogs whose sole function is to provide comfort or emotional support do not qualify as Service Animals. In some cases similarly trained miniature horses may be considered Service Animals.

Emotional Support Animals (ESAs) can be virtually any animal and offer emotional support services to their owners. Although these animals provide comfort to their owners, they do not need to be trained to behave in any particular manner.

Why Is the Type of Assistance Animal Important?

Laws cover where and when assistance animals are permitted to remain with their owners. Service Animals and Emotional Support Animals are NOT treated the same in every situation. The greatest differences occur when bringing assistance animals to public spaces.

- Under the Americans with Disabilities Act (ADA) and Massachusetts General Law c. 272 § 98A, businesses that serve the public, such as restaurants, hotels, retail stores, taxicabs, theaters, concert halls, and sports facilities, are prohibited from discriminating against individuals with disabilities. Among other things, these laws require businesses to allow people with disabilities to bring their Service Animals onto business premises in whatever areas customers are generally allowed.

- The ADA covers only Service Animals, not Emotional Support Animals. Therefore, Emotional Support Animals are not automatically permitted into public spaces along with their owners.

May I Bring My Assistance Animal to a Restaurant or Other Public Place?

It depends. The law is very clear that Service Animals are permitted into public spaces along with their owners. Additionally, facilities are not allowed to charge an additional fee of any kind for the Service Animal. Massachusetts law is clear: "any blind person, deaf or hearing handicapped person, or other physically handicapped person accompanied by a dog guide, shall be entitled to any and all accommodations, advantages, facilities and privileges of all public conveyances, public amusements and places of public accommodation, within the commonwealth, to which persons not accompanied by dogs are entitled."

Of course, any limitations applicable to people also apply to the Service Animal (for example, a Service Animal does not allow an 18 year old person to enter a space limited to persons above 21 years old just because she has a Service Animal). And, in the rare instance a Service Animal is a direct threat to health or safety, the animal can be denied entrance.

Emotional Support Animals are not automatically entitled to these same benefits. Public spaces are not required to allow people and their Emotional Support Animals in together.

Emotional support animals have become common sights on airplanes. But some passengers who are allergic or afraid may feel their rights are being ignored.

The Massachusetts Attorney General's site provides a great resource for those with assistance animals and business owners.

Do I Have to Prove My Assistance Animal Is Required to Stay with Me?

The law is very clear about what business owners may ask you if they are unsure if your animal is a Service Animal. There are only two question permitted:

1. Is the Service Animal required because of a disability?
2. What task(s) does the Service Animal perform?

Importantly, businesses may not ask for documentation or certification that you have a Service Animal. However, if you have a cat or other non-dog or non-miniature horse, you do not have a Service Animal and therefore are not automatically entitled to enter the business—only Service Animals, which must be a dog or miniature horse, are legally allowed to enter with their owners.

May I Bring My Assistance Animals on an Airplane with Me in the Cabin?

The short answer is: yes, you may bring your assistance animal on the airplane with you. There are some important guidelines and distinctions to know about, though.

- Firstly, note that the ADA and another federal law allow assistance animals on an airplane. The Air Carrier Access Act (ACAA) provides guidance that extends beyond the ADA's coverage, which only includes Service Animals. Most importantly, the ACAA allows Emotional Support Animals to board with and remain with their owners on a flight.

- Airlines must permit you to sit in your assigned seat with your assistance animal, unless the animal obstructs an aisle or other area that must remain unobstructed in order to facilitate an emergency evacuation or to comply with FAA regulations. The airline must offer the passenger the opportunity to move with the animal to a seat location in the same class of service, if present on the aircraft, where the animal can be accommodated.

- Airlines are not permitted to charge any additional fees for an assistance animal.

- Airlines are not required to allow unusual or exotic animals if they are too large or heavy, or pose a direct threat to others. Airlines are never required to accept snakes, other reptiles, ferrets, rodents or spiders as service animals

- For Emotional Support Animals only, there are additional steps that must be taken:

  · Passengers with Emotional Support Animals must present the required documentation: a letter from a mental health professional stating that the passenger has a mental health-related disability. The letter must be less than one year old, and be from a mental health professional who is currently treating the passenger.

  · You must also give US airlines 48 hours advance notice if you intend to travel with an Emotional Support Animal.

- Airlines are required to employ Customer Resolution

Professionals, and you should ask to speak to one of them if you experience difficulty with the airline.

- The Department of Transportation operates a toll-free hotline to assist air travelers with disabilities. The hotline assists air travelers with time-sensitive disability-related issues that need to be addressed in "real time." The hours for the hotline are 7am to 5pm EST, Monday through Friday, except federal holidays. Call the hotline at 1-800-778-4838 (voice) or 1-800-455-9880 (TTY) to obtain assistance.

What if My Landlord Has a "No Pets" Policy?

Like with air travel, there is a federal law to provide coverage for assistance animals in housing situations. The Department of Housing and Urban Development released a Notice that discusses how the Fair Housing Act (FHA) and the ADA intersect regarding the use of Service or Emotional Support Animals by persons with disabilities.

- The ADA requires equal access for people with disabilities using trained Service Animals in public accommodations and government facilities. Therefore, people with Service Animals are automatically covered and their Service Animals are allowed to live with them in housing covered by the ADA (public housing).
- According to HUD, "Under the FHA, housing providers have a further obligation [beyond the ADA] to accommodate people with disabilities who, because of their disability, require trained service dogs or other types of assistance animals to perform tasks, provide emotional support, or alleviate the effects of their disabilities."
- Housing providers must evaluate a request for a reasonable accommodation to possess an Assistance Animal— either a Service Animal or an Emotional Support Animal— in a dwelling. The housing provider must consider: (a) Does the person seeking the request

FAST FACT

According to the ADA, an individual with a disability has a physical or mental impairment that substantially limits one or more major life activities.

have a disability? And (b) Does the person making the request have a disability-related need for the assistance animal?

- · Where the answers to questions (a) and (b) are "yes," the FHA requires the housing provider to modify or provide an exception to a "no pets" rule or policy to permit a person with a disability to live with and use an assistance animal(s) in all areas of the premises where persons are normally allowed to go, unless doing so would impose an undue financial and administrative burden or would fundamentally alter the nature of the housing provider's services.

- · Federal laws define a person with a disability as "Any person who has a physical or mental impairment that substantially limits one or more major life activities; has a record of such impairment; or is regarded as having such an impairment." In general, a physical or mental impairment includes hearing, mobility and visual impairments, chronic alcoholism, chronic mental illness, AIDS, AIDS Related Complex, and mental retardation that substantially limits one or more major life activities. Major life activities include walking, talking, hearing, seeing, breathing, learning, performing manual tasks, and caring for oneself.

- A housing provider may not deny a reasonable accommodation request because she or he is uncertain whether or not the person seeking the accommodation has a disability or a disability-related need for an assistance animal.

- Housing providers may ask individuals who have disabilities that are not readily apparent to submit reliable documentation of a disability and their disability-related need for an assistance animal.

A Troubling Trend?

As the *Boston Globe* reported, there is conflict brewing between Service Animals and Emotional Support Animals. Legislation has recently been introduced in Massachusetts (mirroring similar laws in other states) that would punish people for falsely claiming an animal is a Service Animal. A fundamental reason for the tension is that Service

Animals are highly trained, very expensive, and very well-behaved animals that are not pets.

When people bring untrained and badly-behaved animals to public places claiming that they are Service Animals, the resulting confusion and bad feelings reflect poorly on the real Service Animals. Therefore, when people with Service Animals seek access to places clearly covered under the law, business owners are becoming skeptical and giving such people (and their Service Animals) a hard time.

Emotional Support Animals do NOT have the same rights of access as Service Animals. Emotional Support Animals are allowed into far fewer places than Service Animals for a reason: they do not have the formal training and tested temperament to move so freely in society. ESAs provide a tremendous help to their owners, but they do not, yet, qualify as Service Animals and should not be represented as such.

*Entities covered by the ADA must modify their policies to permit miniature horses where reasonable. The regulations set out four assessment factors to assist entities in determining whether miniature horses can be accommodated in their facility. The assessment factors are (1) whether the miniature horse is housebroken; (2) whether the miniature horse is under the owner's control; (3) whether the facility can accommodate the miniature horse's type, size, and weight; and (4) whether the miniature horse's presence will not compromise legitimate safety requirements necessary for safe operation of the facility.

EVALUATING THE AUTHOR'S ARGUMENTS:

In this viewpoint, Massachusetts Society for the Prevention of Cruelty to Animals–Angell discusses the different rights people have when traveling with service animals versus emotional support animals. Why are those two categories different? Should they be? What complications could arise from the current laws and guidelines?

The ESA Loophole Is Worth It

Marisa Meltzer

"Where there's a system, there will always be people trying to exploit that system."

In the following excerpted viewpoint, Marisa Meltzer looks at problems with animals on planes, but she also quotes people who have been helped by a companion animal. She notes that air travel is expensive and uncomfortable, but taking a pet along can make it more bearable. In the end, she asks, is this a good enough reason to allow people to bring their pets on airlines as emotional support animals? Marisa Meltzer is a writer based in New York.

AS YOU READ, CONSIDER THE FOLLOWING QUESTIONS:

1. What is the air carrier definition of an emotional support animal?
2. What problems have ESAs caused on planes?
3. What reasons do people give for bringing an ESA on a plane?

"Prescription Pets: 'I Got a Doctor's Note to Fly with My Dog,'" by Marisa Meltzer, Guardian News & Media Limited, May 12, 2018. Reprinted by permission.

Delta Airlines says it carries more than 250,000 service and support animals annually, an increase of nearly 150% since 2015. The Air Carrier Access Act defines emotional support animals as "any animal that is individually trained or able to provide assistance to a person with a disability; or any animal that assists persons with disabilities by providing emotional support." They're animals that don't have special training (unlike a service animal, such as a guide dog for the blind, that has been trained to perform a task or service for its owner), but are there for psychiatric comfort. They are often cats and dogs, but ducks, turkeys and pigs have been spotted on board.

Unsurprisingly, it's creating havoc on planes. For every dog like mine that snores at my feet during a flight, there are reports of far more unruly behaviour, from cats urinating on drinks trolleys to ducks blocking the aisles. In January, astonished airport passengers filmed a peacock awaiting the green light to board a flight in New Jersey; in February, a student told how she flushed her dwarf hamster down a toilet in panic after an airline refused permission for it to join her flight; in March, a French bulldog died after being put in an overhead locker; last year, a man was hospitalised and had 28 stitches in his face after he was mauled by a support dog in the seat next to him. Delta Airlines reports that incidents such as defecating have nearly doubled since 2016.

I found it almost ludicrously easy to get a certificate for Joan a year after adopting her; I was keen to take her to California to visit my family, so looked for a website that offered online diagnosis.

[...]

That's how it worked for me: a quick pre-screening, payment, a test and a five- to 10-minute phone call with a clinician, describing my history of panic attacks and depression. Then I got a letter that they advertise you can get in less than 48 hours. "We are saying cats or dogs," [CertaPet clinical manager Prairie] Conlon says. "We aren't doing peacocks or anything like that. We also let them know if your animal is aggressive that voids the letter." Does this leave them open to people faking or exaggerating symptoms? "Most of the therapists don't feel people are abusing the system," [US military veteran Erik] Rivera says. "At a company level, we don't think there's a lot of abuse happening. If you can figure out how to stop people from lying, I would like to hear that solution."

Emily Cline is a cheerful 22-year-old social media manager who recently moved to New York after graduating from university in Florida. She's in possession of an ESA letter from CertaPet for her Italian greyhound puppy, Calvin Cline. "I've been flying by myself since I was about five—my parents divorced when I was really little, and it was easier for me to fly back and forth between Dallas and San Antonio, which is a 45-minute flight versus a four-hour drive. I would fly 20 times a year as a child." When she was about 12 and flying, "something didn't click in my brain and I started to think we were in a metal tube in the sky. What if the pilot passes out? I would go over all of these worst-case scenario ideas with panic attacks where I almost felt as if I would have to get off the plane. I have panic disorder. It's not diagnosed, but I know what's going on."

By the time she was in her second year of university, she was given a prescription for Xanax (alprazolam) for her anxiety. "I was surprised how easy it was. I couldn't get an appointment for a school counsellor, but I could get a prescription for Xanax."

The next year, she researched how a dog could help her deal with anxiety. She calls Calvin a Velcro dog. "He's like a third arm, an extension of me. He just sits on my lap, he sleeps with me, he sits on the couch with me, he likes to sit on my shoulder. He's very clingy," Cline says with a giggle. "And what sets them apart is they're really there for you and they depend on you so much for taking care of them. Your brain is so focused on taking care of this tiny, cute dog. That's why flying with them is so great." She recently flew with him and her boyfriend from Florida to New York without an issue. People who may exaggerate their symptoms so they can live with or travel with their pets is the least of our problems, Cline says. "I don't think that's the worst possible thing that's going on in the world."

Like many millennial pet owners, Kim Ring, who is 25 and works in public relations in Denver, Colorado, calls herself a "dog mom." Finn is her two-year-old jack russell terrier mix. "I am one of those annoying people who got a doctor's note so I could bring my dog on a plane. I know it's terrible, but I just wanted to take him home to meet my parents, who have a big backyard and live in St Louis, and didn't want to pay an arm and a leg to do it. I do have anxiety and see a therapist for it, and I asked her to write a note on letterhead designating him an ESA. But the thing is, my dog has so much energy and there's no way he would actually calm me down. I have to heavily medicate him for flights with CBD [cannabidiol-based] dog treats. He was mellow and didn't bark, but he did shake. I feel as if it was almost a selfish thing for me to take him, even though everyone who sat next to me took pictures of him and played with him the whole time."

Taylor Truitt, a veterinarian who owns the Vet Set, a clinic in the leafy Carroll Gardens neighbourhood of Brooklyn, is outspoken on the subject of ESA letters. "I see a potential problem that the people abusing the qualifications for support animals are actually putting people with legitimate working service animals at risk," she said. "I think, for some people, ESAs have a legitimate purpose. My sister is a clinical psychologist who specialises in trauma, sexual abuse and veterans. For some of these people, their dog can save their lives, get them out of the house. It's important to honour them with the respect of what a real ESA is."

Truitt has seen evidence of malpractice. "One of my clients brought in their new frenchie puppy this weekend," she says. "The breeder flew her up from Florida, and in the packet of paperwork he inadvertently left his letter from his therapist stating this eight-week-old puppy was an ESA to help him with his stress and anxiety. It was one of those form letters you can purchase online. I can't imagine what special training an eight-week-old puppy can have to help with stress except congenital cuteness. I've been on a flight where this is out of control, with a dog running down the aisles and another barking. Are they going to emergency land the plane if your dog is having, say, respiratory issues? Probably not, so another question is what are you subjecting your pet to. We could use some etiquette."

Many people suffer from severe anxiety when they travel by air. Are ESAs the answer?

Delta Airlines responded to the recent increase in ESAs by changing its policy for service and support animals. Customers need not only a letter but clearance from a veterinarian or immunisation record and a confirmation of animal training. The US Department of Transportation says that unusual service animals (ie anything other than a dog or a cat) will be evaluated on a case-by-case basis, but it's at the discretion of the airline to exclude animals that are too large or perceived as a threat. Delta prohibits ferrets, snakes, goats, "farm poultry," hedgehogs and beasts with tusks, for example.

It was a particularly flamboyant animal that ruffled feathers this year. In January, Brooklyn-based performance artist Ventiko was not allowed to take a United Airlines flight with her support animal, a large peacock named Dexter, whose elaborate Instagram presence features photos of him cuddling with naked women and hanging out on thrones. She was photographed by an incredulous fellow passenger as she tried to board the plane with Dexter at Newark and the story immediately went viral on social media. I emailed Ventiko asking about her story and, after a delay, she replied: "My apologies for taking a few days to respond. The entire situation over the past few months has been a bit traumatic. Slow responses is one of the residual effects." We then spoke for nearly an hour, during which I found her a fairly sympathetic character who is just trying to do right by her peacock companion animal, a bird she adopted after his mate and their chicks were eaten by a predator in Florida. He's bonded to her, and she seems almost uncannily devoted to him. But she decided she didn't want to get any further death threats, and no longer wanted to speak on the record.

Last year, on a Delta flight to California, an Alabama man named Marlin Jackson was assigned a window seat. In a subsequent statement, his attorney J. Ross Massey said, "He saw a large dog on the middle seat that he had to cross over to get to his seat. After he goes to buckle his seatbelt, the dog attacks him. The owner yanked the dog back, but it broke free and went into a second attack, which resulted in Mr. Jackson needing 28 stitches. It was reportedly an ESA."

In the wake of the publicity the case received, Massey has received "dozens if not hundreds of people calling me about a badly behaving dog on a plane," he tells me. People contacting him with stories of ESA pets touching them, crawling on them or defecating at their feet are unfortunate, possibly disturbing, events, but hardly warrant the law, he says. "It's a nuanced situation. Ultimately, the airlines will have to police themselves. I'm not sure how quickly the government is going to act."

One group that would like to see a change is the service animal community—people such as Laura Falteisek, 64, a retired marketing manager who lives in northern California with five pedigree, elaborately groomed poodles that she has trained: Titan came first, then Jodie, his niece; the rest—Ava, Chin Chin and Sequin—are Jodie's from litters with two different sires. Falteisek had a mutt as a child that she had wanted to be a service animal after reading about Helen Keller. "I think I only taught him 'left' and 'right,'" she says with a laugh. She was drawn to poodles because "they're tall, light on their feet, don't shed and are smart."

Her dogs respond to the command "bring," because she is unable to bend well and has general mobility issues due to past injuries following an equestrian accident. "They reach for me and pick up stuff," Falteisek says. "They could pick up a coin off the floor. They'll do it all day long." Titan, for example, can brace her if she stumbles. "If I drop my cane, he gets it for me. He's great at helping me with stairs." He can bark on command, indicate steps and barriers, and understands the command "help me." People want to interact with the poodles when they are essentially at work. "I was at a grocery store in so much pain looking down at yoghurt, and someone goes, 'Oh, look, it's a poodle!' I didn't want to respond and I didn't want to talk to anybody right then. They have vests that say, this is a service dog, not a pet."

Her worry is that the bad reputation some support animals are getting will give all service animals a bad name. Someone told Falteisek she was considering getting an ESA letter for her dogs because, "I just can't leave them in the car." She explains that properly training a service dog is incredibly expensive and complicated, "and yet you'll see people with these snarling, snapping dogs going everywhere with their owners."

Animals are commonly used in therapy roles. In the UK, therapy animals have been an established idea for decades—Pets As Therapy is a charity founded in 1983—and therapy dogs are common visitors in hospitals, care homes and schools. The charity Support Dogs provides dogs to support people with autism, as well as seizure alert dogs.

Although ESAs don't exist in the UK, there are cases where pets have proved to be vitally therapeutic. Ellie Taylor, 20, who is from

Rowley Regis in the West Midlands, found that her pet rabbits helped her through a difficult childhood. "When I was 13 in 2011, I lost my grandad suddenly and was also having problems at school with bullying. I wasn't able to cope and became ill with anorexia." Her mother got her professional help and she left school to concentrate on her recovery. "I still felt as if I was in hell and that nothing around me could possibly make me feel better. When my mum could see I was slowly improving, she agreed for me to have a rabbit, because she felt that if I had responsibilities, it would help me to get better."

Taylor felt excited for the first time in two years. She got two rabbits, Roary and Tiger, and because she still wasn't back in school full-time, spent nearly all her time with them. "They comforted me when I felt like I had no one and gave me some normality back by looking after them. It was weird that an animal could make you feel like this and take the pain away, but the pain began to ease and I felt like myself again." Tiger died, and she and Roary got through that loss together. Where she lives now has a no-pets policy, but she fought to keep Roary with her and won, something she wouldn't have had to do if she could have him officially recognised as a support animal. In 2016, vet charity PDSA honoured Roary with a "commendation for devotion" for his support.

It's indisputable that animals provide comfort and support to their owners, but whether that means they should be certified in this manner is less clear: where there's a system, there will always be people trying to exploit that system.

Animals can be so much better at calming us down than humans. Take me, for example. Do I have anxiety? Sure. A history of depression? Yes. Insomnia? Almost nightly. And, like more than half my peers in New York, I have been in therapy. And the thing is, Joan does bring me endless comfort. After a terse email exchange with a colleague, taking her on a walk or just petting her on the sofa are effective balms for encroaching panic attacks. No one would look at me and think, "That woman needs a dog just to get through the day," but, in a sense, I do.

Are we American pet owners needy? Yes, and owners like me who bring their pets while travelling are certainly entitled, but the overall indignity of travel has brought us here, too. It already feels like a free-for-all in the sky. If there are screaming children on every flight, and tiny spaces with not much legroom that make everyone uncomfortable, and they're going to charge you for bottles of water and checking in a bag, what harm is there in bringing a pet that soothes you?

When my flight touched down in San Francisco, Joan woke from her slumber and soon ran into the arms of my waiting mother. When Mum asked about who I was dating, or when my dad wanted to complain about politics, I could tell them I was going to take Joan for a walk to the beach. For once, I wasn't acting like a sullen teenager when interacting with my family. That respite, not to mention saving hundreds of dollars on boarding Joan while I was out of town, meant that loophole or not, it was totally worth it.

EVALUATING THE AUTHOR'S ARGUMENTS:

Viewpoint author Marisa Meltzer ultimately decides that bringing her pet on a plane as an ESA is worthwhile. Does Meltzer offer enough support to convince you of her viewpoint? Whose rights and comfort should be prioritized, the person needing an ESA, other people on the plane, or the airline companies? Why?

Viewpoint 4

COVID-19 Presents Obstacles for People Who Use Service Animals

Virginie Abat-Roy

"Our society de facto obliges people with disabilities to fight for their essential rights, such as accessibility."

In the following viewpoint, Virginie Abat-Roy explores how the COVID-19 pandemic changed things for people with service animals. Guide dogs are trained to help people with daily life, but COVID-19 changed daily life for everyone. Service animals have not been trained for the new realities, while business owners rarely consider the special needs of people with service animals. Virginie Abat-Roy studies animal assisted therapy at the University of Ottawa.

AS YOU READ, CONSIDER THE FOLLOWING QUESTIONS:
1. What is ableism?
2. What challenges do people and their service animals face due to COVID-19?
3. What would help people with service animals to handle these changes?

While browsing through a Facebook group for guide, mobility and service dog recipients, a post by one of the members jumped out at me. "Did you dare to go out with your dog?" it asked. "Are you able to go out of your home?" Since the early days of the COVID-19 crisis in March, many have had their eyes glued to the news and are following government guidelines. But in all this turmoil, have we forgotten about citizens living with a disability?

I am a doctoral student at the University of Ottawa and a resource teacher for suspended or expelled students. I specialize in the areas of inclusion and service dogs. My research project allowed me to have Toulouse, an assistance dog from the Mira Foundation trained specifically for my special needs students. Since March 2019, she has been accompanying me everywhere and has helped me discover a reality that I didn't expect.

As a researcher in this field, I am fortunate to have access to networks of assistance dog beneficiaries. With this article, I would like to offer them a public voice in order to draw a portrait of their reality since the beginning of the COVID-19 crisis.

A Lack of Accessibility

Ableism is the word used to describe the extent of multi-dimensional discrimination against people living with disabilities. People with working dogs are victims of it on a daily basis. Indeed, our society is designed for citizens without disabilities and de facto obliges people with disabilities to fight for their essential rights, such as accessibility, despite the provisions included in the Canadian Charter of Rights and Freedoms and the Canadian Human Rights Act, which "guarantee equal rights and freedom from discrimination to persons with disabilities."

Normally, working dogs accompany these individuals and facilitate their daily life. However, since the beginning of the COVID-19 crisis, the barriers to accessibility have never been so great.

The Risks of Exclusion Are Increasing

Anne-Marie Bourcier is visually impaired and received her third guide dog from the Mira Foundation. With her dog, Machine, she routinely takes the bus and subway to go shopping or have lunch with a friend. Autonomy is the watchword for this duo. However, since the pandemic, they no longer go out in public. She wrote me a long email to let me know about her new reality.

> *I don't see how I could be autonomous with my guide dog in a grocery store. Where do the arrows start? Where are the sinks for washing hands? Am I going to graze someone? Are we going to make a mistake in the aisles? Is someone going to help me once I get there? My guide dog is used to going straight into the store. If we go in, will they tell us to get out and get in line? I think it's quite complex.*

These questions remain unanswered for Bourcier and many others. The physical obstacles are major, especially for a dog that has not been trained to deal with the health crisis and prevention measures.

While we might assume that people give priority to those living with disabilities, the opposite is true. For example, another guide dog recipient explains that he often has to avoid people who do not give way to him.

Fast Fact

It is estimated that 10% of people in the US have a medical condition that could be considered an invisible disability.

Dogs and Social Distancing

Added to this are situations where the disability is not visible and the public believes that the dog is in training. Awareness campaigns on social distancing have been conducted by the CNIB Foundation.

In addition to the physical obstacles, there are also

The outbreak of COVID-19 brought new challenges to people who rely on service animals.

psychological obstacles. "At the hospital, I need my dog and my partner for my MRI. I had to negotiate for entry," says Geneviève, a traction dog recipient. The mask makes it hard for her to breathe and she has to constantly adjust her tone of voice to give instructions to her dog. "I feel badly about taking her in. With the distancing, there is a fear of people and sometimes small alleys. I'm scared to go out again."

Thus, the risk of social isolation is amplified for service dog users who have to stay at home and forget about their routine.

The Other Side of the Coin

Despite the difficulties, there are some positive experiences. Several beneficiaries are happy that the implementation of social distancing rules means nobody tries to pet their dog, which usually happens several times per outing. This distraction may cause the animal to make a mistake, which could put the safety of the user at risk.

In fact, all of them are grateful to have a companion during this crisis. In spite of the isolation, the beneficiaries can count on the reassuring presence of their animal. Marie Eve Leduc is the mother of a child diagnosed with an autism spectrum disorder (ASD) who has an assistance dog. She is relieved to have had Amhara for her boy.

> *During confinement, Amhara proved her worth. Since Arthur hasn't returned to school, he's spending a lot more time with her! He spends long moments holding on to her, talking to her, petting her.... The change in his habits went well, thanks to our dog!*

After several months of confinement, the reopening of stores has also made going out again easier.

Solutions Exist

As the process of deconfinement continues in Canada, many recipients are concerned that they will be overlooked as the measures rarely take into consideration Canadians living with disabilities. A few solutions are therefore suggested for them, including priority entry at all times, reserved hours and a shopping assistance service.

Masks with a transparent screen or visors to allow deaf or hard of hearing people to read lips would be necessary in essential services, particularly at the reception desk. Finally, distancing could become permanent around recipients of working dogs.

In this wave of change, it is up to us to seize the opportunity to make our society a more accessible place.

EVALUATING THE AUTHOR'S ARGUMENTS:

Viewpoint author Virginie Abat-Roy explores extra challenges brought on by COVID-19. How could businesses and individuals help support people with service animals during times like these? Should special access and other considerations be required or optional? How can businesses let people know what is available to them?

You Can Train Your Own Service Dog

Margie Rucker

"A service vest on a 6.5 pound dog can be a hard sell when facing a storekeeper who insists he's fake."

In the following viewpoint, Margie Rucker describes life using her service dog to help with an invisible disability. She trained a dog that she already had as a pet to do specific tasks related to her mental illness. Because her dog is small, people sometimes doubt he is a true service animal. However, the author argues that this type of dog is ideal for certain disabilities.

AS YOU READ, CONSIDER THE FOLLOWING QUESTIONS:
1. How long does it take to train a service dog?
2. What training does a dog need to become a service dog?
3. What are the advantages to a purebred dog as a service dog, according to the author?

"The Truth About Service Dogs," by Margie Rucker, The American Kennel Club, Inc., March 18, 2015. Reprinted by permission.

Piper is my Service Dog. Piper does not look like the typical Service Dog. Piper's undeniable charm, stature, and jolly demeanor elicits amused skepticism and, occasionally, unkind comments. Over time I've learned that all responses are opportunities for me to provide accurate information and to advocate for the lawful and appropriate use of Service Dogs.

When communicating with a doubting public, an understanding of the legal definition of Service Dog and its application in practice (what kinds of tasks do Service Dogs perform?) is paramount. It is equally important to understand the difference between a Service Dog and an Emotional Support Dog (ESD). Being able to discuss the minimum standards of behavior as well as owner training versus professional training are important.

Piper rarely fails to convince even the most skeptical that he is indeed a Service Dog. He wears his little service vest with pride, and takes his role seriously. He is at my side on public transportation, stays to the left rear wheel of my grocery cart, accompanies me on nail appointments and doctor/dentist appointments and trots confidently through Costco. If a store or business owner questions his role, he stands quietly by my side as I reply to the two questions they may legally ask, "Is he a service dog?" and "What tasks does he perform?" Most of the time those interactions are pleasant.

The truth is I am one of many individuals who suffer from what has been called an "invisible" disability. I have mental health limitations that interfere with my ability to fully perform and participate in major life activities. All my life my dogs have helped me to overcome my depression and anxiety disorder. In recent years, I have come to understand my disability and, with the help of my doctors and therapist, have formalized the role my dog plays in my life.

The Department of Justice's Disability Rights Section document entitled ADA Requirements: Service Animals, dated July 12, 2011 states, "Service animals are defined as dogs that are individually trained to work or perform tasks for people with disabilities." The document provides examples of disabilities such as blindness, deafness, mobility impairments, and more invisible disabilities such as psychiatric conditions including PTSD. Service Dogs are also paired with people suffering from other invisible disabilities such as autism,

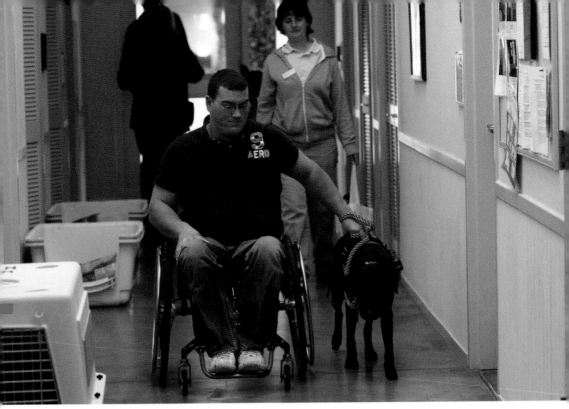

Is one service dog more valid than another? And who gets to make that determination?

diabetes and epilepsy. The document points out, "Dogs whose sole function is to provide comfort or emotional support (Emotional Support Dog) do not qualify as service animals under the ADA." There are some shared rights of access for ESD dogs and their owners, however those rights are more limited. The key to the difference is a Service Dog requires specific task training that "must be directly related to the persons disability."

Choosing to use a Service Dog brings immediate visibility to invisible disabilities, particularly when choosing to use a Psychiatric Service Dog. There is still a stigma, as well as a "get hold of yourself" mentality associated with mental health issues that makes me hesitate to own my difficulties in such a public way. No one in my professional circle, or the public I dealt with daily during my career as an educator, was aware of my past hospitalizations, the fact that I was on medication or that I stayed in counseling for the majority of my career. My mental health struggles have been difficult for me to face, and own. It has taken me almost my entire adult life to accept this part of myself. My husband's loving support and respect has helped. Choosing to use a Psychiatric Service Dog, I believe, is part of that loving acceptance of myself I want to foster. Piper therefore now, upon command, performs tasks to interrupt my emotional anxiety episodes and bring me back to equilibrium. He also, among others tasks, is trained to distract me from engaging in behaviors that are unhealthy. Piper merrily performs these tasks, while at the same time inadvertently directing attention away from me to himself. I am grateful, as I much prefer to remain in his sweet shadow. As per ADA requirements, the tasks he performs are directly related to my medical condition.

Most people are surprised to learn that under federal law, an individual can task train their own dog. In fact, if the individual is capable, it can be a preferred method of obtaining a service dog. There are a multitude of organizations springing up across the country who are supplying Service Dogs, however, it behooves the individual to adopt a "buyer beware" attitude toward some of these organizations. (I will address minimum training requirements and recommended hours of training below.) Many individual trainers and organizations have earned and deserve great respect. Canine Companions for Independence, for instance, has been around for many years and deserves its fine reputation. Another organization, Can Do Canines, located in New Hope, Minnesota, has been providing Type 1 diabetics trained service dogs and even hosts training seminars for organizations that can in turn use their training methods. Nevertheless, the requests for Service Dogs far exceeds the supply. Many people, unwilling to wait for what sometimes amounts to years on waiting lists, turn to ADI accredited service animal organizations such as Top Dog, located in Arizona. Top Dog teaches disabled persons to train their own service dog. Other individuals seek out non-profit training organizations, for-profit centers, or contact local trainers. Many, if they are able, start training their dogs themselves.

FAST FACT

The International Association of Assistance Dog Partners (IAADP) recommends 120 hours of schooling, including outings, over a period of 6 months or more.

My situation is not uncommon for those who choose to owner-train their own Service Dog. I had prior work experience at a dog training center. I already owned a dog who had been my pet for two years, and who was intensely focused on me (an important quality). I discussed my intentions with my physician. He agreed to support task training my dog to meet my specific medical condition. I did all the initial groundwork myself and then worked with a local trainer to fine tune the training.

Piper responded to the work with joy. He seemed thrilled to have yet another avenue for pleasing me. There were, however, challenges. Piper had grown accustomed as a pet, to interacting frequently with the public during our walks. He now had to learn to stay focused and at heel by my side. This has actually been tough on both of us as I take great joy in sharing my little buddy, particularly with children. We still frequently stop to answer questions, but now he gazes from a distance while on a sit command, no matter how tempted he is by an often adoring public. I make sure to give him lots of pats and praise for his restraint.

The International Association of Assistance Dog Partners (IAADP) (http://www.iaadp.org) is an outstanding resource for anyone with an interest in Service Dogs. IAADP regularly advocates for and is involved in Service Animal issues and legislation. For instance, they have long been active advocating for access for Service Dogs and their partners with US Housing and Urban Development (HUD) and the Department of Transportation. IAADP not only puts out a newsletter and maintains a comprehensive website, they also make available webcast workshops, and provide peer support and advocacy information. I found their Minimum Training Standards for Public Access (available on their website) guidelines invaluable. They recommend 120 hours of schooling over a period of six months or more, 30 hours of which should be devoted to outings, as well as a set of obedience tasks similar to the AKC Good Canine Companion criteria, and of course the specific disability related tasks. Their section on Assistance Dog Tasks helped me to understand the types of tasks to help mitigate my condition that would meet the ADA's criteria.

IAADP provides free of charge a 2013 webcast entitled Assessing Dogs for a Service Dog Career. That video identifies three areas to consider when assessing a dog's suitability for service. Those important considerations are health, temperament and aptitude. Piper met the criteria in the webcast seminar.

There are important pros and cons to using a Papillon as a Service Dog. A service vest on a 6.5 pound dog can be a hard sell when facing a storekeeper who insists he's fake. A Seeing Eye dog his size would be a recipe for disaster, and he certainly could never pull someone in a wheelchair. His size, however, can also be a positive thing. He fits easily under my feet in movie theaters, goes through turnstiles with ease, and can put all four feet on one step of an escalator going up or down. (He's confused when escalators are broken. He just stands there.) Seriously though, a Papillon is perfect for people with hearing loss, diabetes, epilepsy, and for my situation. They are smart, agile, temperamentally suited for the work, and long-lived.

IAADP's recommended criteria for assessing suitability for service, plus my own experience, lead me to advocate strongly for the use of purebred dogs, large or small, obtained through reputable and responsible breeders, rather than using rescue or animal shelter dogs as service dogs. I know my opinion on this matter will rattle some cages in the dog world, but having owned several rescue dogs myself, I can attest to the fact that health histories, particularly for known inherited disorders, are extremely important when considering suitability for service. Invest your time, emotional energy, and money in a dog whose risk of inherited disorders has been monitored through careful breeding and screening. Purebred dogs offer a more predictable population to choose from for the other two important qualities necessary in a service dog, temperament and aptitude. For hundreds of years dogs have been bred for specific aptitudes and temperaments. Purebred dogs offer us a gold mine of breeds from which to select from for predictable intelligence, aptitude, and temperament. You just can't get all those known qualities in mixed breeds, or even in purebred rescues with unknown pedigrees. I am not suggesting mixed breeds and purebred rescues can't be excellent service dogs. Many are currently serving in that capacity at this very moment. I am saying health, aptitude and temperament are more predictable in responsibly bred pure breeds.

Piper is out of stock bred for soundness, intelligence, longevity of life, aptitude, temperament and type. His dam and sire are purebred Papillons. Piper was a year-and-half old when his breeder decided to place him with me. When she placed Piper with me, neither of us knew Piper would some day become a Service Dog. We have stayed in regular contact and she has been appraised (sometimes daily) on his successes and challenges. Her support has been invaluable to me. She maintains that one of Piper's strongest characteristics is an almost intuitive ability to read a person's needs and respond to them. This trait best predicted his suitability for the unexpected role he is currently filling.

Perhaps an event for which Piper is not task trained illustrates best his suitability. I suffer from frequent and vivid nightmares. Sometimes I'll go out to my living room in the middle of the night and watch the flames in my wood stove to calm down. Well one evening I dozed off in the living room, only to go straight back into a nightmarish vivid dream. This time, however, I was woken up by a warm tongue and a worried little face intent on reassuring me. He continues to practice his self taught task, staying within "tongues" reach nightly.

In the end, Piper provides the public with a positive "in person" (or rather "in dog") encounter with a Service Dog. He invites inquiry and examination in part because of his stature, charm, demeanor and undeniable good looks. I am blessed with his companionship and service.

EVALUATING THE AUTHOR'S ARGUMENTS:

Viewpoint author Margie Rucker discusses some of the pros and cons involved when someone with a disability trains their own pet as a Service Dog. Does this seem like a better or worse option than getting a dog trained by an organization? What factors might someone consider in their choice?

Chapter 3

What Are Some of the Challenges with Assistance Animals?

Miniature horses can be trained to act as guide dogs for the blind.

Viewpoint 1

Consider the Animals' Health and Welfare

"Clients make unrealistic demands on their animals in an attempt to ensure maximum animal benefit for themselves or a loved one."

Myrna Milani

In the following viewpoint, Myrna Milani argues that while many people value service, emotional support, and therapy animals for their help to humans, the physical and emotional health of the animal may be neglected. At times, veterinarians may discover that owners' needs and wants are interfering with the animal patients' care. Vets may need to work with physicians to develop plans that keep both human and animal patients healthy. Myrna Milani is a veterinarian who has written books and articles on the relationship between pets and their owners.

AS YOU READ, CONSIDER THE FOLLOWING QUESTIONS:
1. What does SAESA stand for?
2. Why is it tricky for veterinarians to ask about their human clients' health issues?
3. Why might veterinarians and doctors need to work together to make sure support animals are healthy?

"Emerging SAESA Communication Challenges," by Myrna Milani, Canadian Veterinary Medical, October 2016. Reprinted by permission.

When articles, books, movies, and other media events describing the human physical and mental health benefits of animal companionship first appeared, Dr. Lorakis applauded their appearance because she believed these representations reflected her own views. Her more practical side also initially viewed this all-positive view of the human-animal bond as good for business. However, over time she noticed several disturbing trends that created problems for her and her partner, Dr. Bussino.

One of these may strike a responsive chord in those puzzled by the meaning of the SAESA acronym. It refers to the service, assistance, or emotional support animals used by disabled people. A collective term was chosen because, although multiple organizations and legislative bodies may assign specific definitions and credentials to the animals in each group, there are none upon which all agree. Additionally, members of the public, media, and even those who train or employ these animals may use the terms interchangeably. Consequently, the first communication challenge Drs. Lorakis and Bussino face is accepting that any expectations they maintain regarding the fitness and duties of animals bearing a service, assistance, or emotional support label might not match those of the animal's owner or even the human medical professional who may have prescribed the animal.

Additionally, their interest in and concern for animal health and welfare causes the practitioners to define the bond as a biological and emotional connection between the person and the animal. The fact that most of the SAESA representations of it position these animals as a means to a human end instead of as living beings with their own physical and mental health needs troubles them.

"Until relatively recently, all of the service animals we saw were carefully bred, selected, and well-trained animals, primarily for the physically disabled," explains Dr. Bussino. "The dogs and their handlers worked together as a team and the good health and behavior of the animal was considered essential for the success of both. That's not necessarily the way it is now."

Dr. Bussino refers to the increased numbers of professionally or self-prescribed SAESA animals their practice now sees. Unlike the service dogs he remembers, many of these animals benefit people with hidden disabilities. ("Hidden disabilities" are those physical and mental impairments that are not immediately apparent. See http://www.disabled-world.com/disability/types/invisible/ for a discussion and list of these.) Consequently, the veterinarians are apt to learn about the animal's status after-the-fact. Consider the following stressful situations such after-the-fact revelations may generate.

Scenario 1: The client tells the veterinarian that he needs his dog to stabilize him during intermittent emotional breakdowns associated with post-traumatic stress disorder (PTSD). Because of this, he cannot possibly leave the animal for dental prophylaxis, including the removal of several badly infected teeth that are undermining the dog's health.

Scenario 2: A client presents a previously well-behaved and relaxed pet dog which now displays signs of anxiety, lick granulomas on both front legs, and intermittent loose stool and diarrhea. When asked about any changes in the household, the client explains that she now cares for her 5-year-old autistic grandson. She also notes that she considers the dog a godsend because the highly active child spends several hours daily chasing and "rough-housing" with the dog. This gives her a respite from her caregiving duties.

In these scenarios, clients make unrealistic demands on their animals in an attempt to ensure what those people consider maximum animal benefit for themselves or a loved one. This brings us to the first practitioner communications challenge. Given the growing number of disabled persons in general, practitioners should possess knowledge of national, provincial, or local laws that may limit how much they can ask their clients about their disabilities and the status of their SAESA. Admittedly, even when such laws exist they may be vague or conflicting. (The United States federal and state disability laws are good examples of this.) Consequently, it is better to gain this knowledge before situations involving SAESA arise than attempt to gain this information at that time.

FAST FACT

Invisible or hidden disabilities can include chronic pain, chronic fatigue, mental illness, chronic dizziness, sleep disorders, and diabetes if those conditions impair normal activities.

The second communication challenge involves the

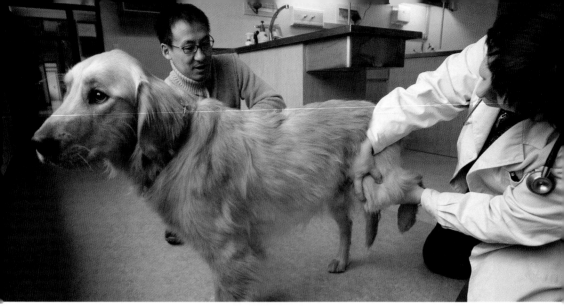

Veterinarians may work in conjunction with physicians to ensure that the health and limitations of service animals are being considered.

acquisition of more detailed information regarding any disabled client limitations veterinarians may need to take into account when addressing SAESA health or behavioral issues. Logic says that, if the animal was prescribed by a human healthcare professional, that person's input would be invaluable. However, in order for this to occur 3 things must happen. First, the client must be willing to give the veterinarian permission to contact the professional. Second, the professional must be willing to share information about his/her patient or client with the veterinarian. And third, the human healthcare professional must be aware of and actively involved in the presence of the SAESA in the client's household.

Applying this to the first scenario, Dr. Lorakis begins by acknowledging how important the dog is to her client's well-being.

"That's why it's so important to keep him healthy," she continues. "Would you be willing to give me permission to contact your healthcare provider so we can come up with a plan that allows me to remove Zuzu's infected teeth without causing you or her unnecessary stress?"

In situations in which healthcare professionals give the same careful attention to the prescription of SAESA that they do to the prescription of drugs, veterinarians and human healthcare professionals can discuss the best way to ensure quality human and animal health and well-being. After gaining her client's permission, Dr. Lorakis calls the healthcare provider, explains how the dog's condition is interfering with the animal's ability to provide reliable support for her owner, and enlists the provider's help. Between the two of them, they formulate a solution that meets canine and client needs.

Sometimes, however, human healthcare professionals may prescribe animals without giving their patients or their caregivers guidance regarding the proper breeding, selection, training, care and treatment of the animal. While some of these professionals simply do not realize all the time and effort that goes into ensuring the success of an SAESA and want to learn more, others do not. Veterinarians and those in the first group can engage in mutually beneficial discussions that represent One Health at its grass roots, practical best. Communicating with those in the second group, on the other hand, can be more challenging.

In the second scenario, the healthcare provider tells Dr. Bussino that she mentioned the use of dogs as support animals for children with autism spectrum disorder (ASD) only to relax her patient's grandmother.

"That was her first visit with her grandson and I only did it to make her feel more comfortable," the therapist explained. "When she mentioned she liked dogs, the memory of an article about their use in some pediatric cases of ASD just popped into my head. I personally don't prescribe animals for any reason. But if I did, I'd never prescribe one for an unpredictably violent child with poor impulse control like her grandson."

In this scenario, Dr. Bussino receives no support from the healthcare provider regarding how to resolve the canine part of the problem. However, he does learn more about the grandson's disability and that his client misinterpreted the therapist's casual dog-related remarks. The child's therapist also gives the veterinarian permission to share her comments with the child's grandmother who he already knew loved her dog and never would do anything intentionally to harm the animal. When he presents this information to his client, he also provides information about setting up regular visits from a certified therapy dog-handler team that would benefit her grandson, her, and her dog.

Finally, practitioners may encounter animals that belong to a growing population of fraudulent SAESA bearing fake credentials readily available online. In a worst-case scenario, a fight erupts in the waiting room when a dog wearing a vest that identifies him as an emotional support dog lunges and grabs a smaller dog by the neck. Dogs which behave like this obviously are not legitimate SAESA regardless of what their vests or credentials say. Any special consideration legally due any SAESA moreover only applies to well-behaved animals. In this situation, Drs. Lorakis and Bussino's first obligation is to ensure the safety of their other clients and patients and attend to the injured dog. To that end, Dr. Bussino politely but firmly asks the owner of the aggressive dog to leave and call for an appointment to discuss her animal's behavior at some future time. Simultaneously Dr. Lorakis whisks away the distraught owner and canine victim for a thorough examination and any needed treatment.

Few veterinarians question the use of properly selected and trained SAESA when paired with disabled people whose needs the animals can fulfill in a manner that does not compromise the animal's physical and mental well-being. When mismatches result in harm to the animal or others are harmed by the animal, however, it becomes the veterinarian's responsibility to do their best to rectify the situation.

EVALUATING THE AUTHOR'S ARGUMENTS:

Viewpoint author Myrna Milani addresses the role of support animals from the viewpoint of animal health and well-being. Should animals be allowed to suffer in order to benefit humans in need? Why or why not? If so, how much?

Pets Can Have Mental Health Issues, Too

Amber M. Snyder

"Yes, as crazy as this may sound I wanted to keep the dog that was triggering my PTSD."

In the following viewpoint, Amber M. Snyder describes her experience adopting a dog who had a traumatic start in life. The dog's apparent PTSD triggered the author's own anxiety and PTSD, and his behavior led to accidents. While these issues were hard to handle, the author found ways to help the dog. In the process, she helped herself and became more accepting of her own issues. Amber M. Snyder is an abuse survivor who blogs about her recovery and her life with mental illnesses.

AS YOU READ, CONSIDER THE FOLLOWING QUESTIONS:
1. Why might an animal develop PTSD?
2. What are some ways an animal with PTSD might react?
2. Did this author find that her pet helped or hindered her own mental health?

I think I wrote in one of my posts that my new dog, Moo, who is my Emotional Support Animal (ESA), has issues. When I first got him, I was living by myself since we were in the process of moving and my parents had already moved into the condo. So it was just the two of us. He loved me—I'd just saved him from shelter living and I liked him. I can't say I loved him at that time because I was still grieving my old dog's death, but he was something I could hold on to.

A little background on him so you get why I say he has PTSD. He was born on the streets of the Bahamas, one of thousands of dogs that run wild there. At three-four weeks old someone poisoned food and left it out for the wild dogs (instead of getting their pets fixed this is how people deal with the wild dogs in the islands). Moo's mom got ahold of some of the poisoned food and died. At this point he had to fend for himself or die too. For two or three weeks after his mom died, he and his two siblings were on the streets alone, people chasing them, either to scare them off or to catch them, before he was caught. Then he went through being shipped to the USA, going through quarantine, going to the vet for things like shots, microchips, and getting fixed. He was paraded out weekly for adoption shows where it was loud, and people were passing him around, at which point it just got too traumatic for him. Then I found him at one of those shows and he sat in my lap so quietly I took him home thinking he was the "ONE" for me.

FAST FACT

Post-traumatic stress disorder (PTSD) is triggered by experiencing or witnessing a terrifying event. Symptoms may include flashbacks, nightmares, anxiety, and sensitivity to loud noises or an accidental touch.

Then I started picking up on things. First, he followed me EVERYWHERE, I couldn't move without Moo being right there. Which led to me tripping over him. Which is a problem because I'm already prone to accidents and falling. While we were still in the house he'd crawl into my lap whenever someone was in the house. If it was a man he'd try digging so he could get behind my back to hide. The

What happens when an emotional support animal has emotional problems of its own?

only one who could touch him was me and my nieces when they'd visit. Anyone over three foot tall that wasn't me, he'd freak out, run away, hid, pee himself or play dead, sometimes all of them at once. Once we moved to the condo, Moo started hiding under my bed. Anytime he heard or saw someone that wasn't me, off he'd go, and he wouldn't come out unless it was just him and I, and the door was closed. I actually had to move things around so he had a place to hide. Otherwise he'd get stuck under there and I couldn't get him out.

The condo move was already stressful for me, and now I was dealing with a freaked out puppy/dog on top of it. I hate to say this and I never would have even thought it before, but I was close to returning him to the shelter. Up until this time I believed that once you take on a dog that dog is your responsibility for life—either theirs or yours, but I started to wonder if our parting wouldn't be better for both of us since he was driving my anxiety levels over-the-top big time. There was just one problem—by the time his PTSD became really noticeable we'd had three months of just him and I time in the house before we sold it, and I was attached plus I was still grieving the loss of one dog and didn't want to lose another.

So I had to come up with ways of treating his PTSD so he'd stop triggering mine. Yes, as crazy as this may sound I wanted to keep the dog that was triggering my PTSD. The first step was realizing that he had problems. The next was finding a way to work on his problems that not only helped him but didn't trigger me. His biggest problem was people, guess what, so is mine. I found out that he loves being around other dogs though, so where could he be around both dogs and people? Pet stores were out cause I can't take them—too crowded and closed in, and noises. I then started looking into dog training classes. They were ok for a start, but I really only did them because my dog need basic training and he liked them. I on the other hand didn't like them so much, because well I was stuck inside with people and I felt weird about leaving in the middle of a class when I started getting panicky. The next thing we tried was the off-leash dog park. This worked for both of us. He got to be with and play with dogs, I was outside so I felt less trapped, and I could move or leave whenever I started getting panicky. It took almost six months of two-to-three times a week visits to the park before Moo would even go near another human, another six months before he'd let a woman pet him. We've just reached the two year mark and he's finally going up to people (men and women) and letting them pet him. At home he's gotten a lot better too. Most of my extended family he likes and most of my friends. He's still scared of strangers, especially men, which he growls at before coming to jump on my lap. He still doesn't bark but I'm ok with that. I still have to watch for signs he's nervous around someone, usually I let him in my bedroom when that happens, but now he no longer feels the need to hide under the bed.

He has other little things that he still does, like he won't eat from his bowl if you are near him. If you come near him and he's eating he leaves. So I feed him at night so he can eat while we sleep. If you give him a treat he runs off and hides to eat it. He has to be under the covers in my bed went it rains, thunders or there are fireworks or other loud noises or he cries. It is emotionally painful when he cries. And if I'm gone for longer than four hours he starts looking out the windows and pacing from door to door looking for me. Then when I get home he follows me around again. He has horrible nightmares but so do I so we keep each other company and calm each other down.

I know I said early I thought of returning Moo because of his issues but I can truly say that I'm thankful I didn't. I'm also thankful every day that when I went looking for a new dog, God saw fit to give me Moo. Not only do I understand him better than most people would, but he also helps me understand and be more accepting of myself and my issues, by dealing with and accept his. And I can say now without a doubt that he enriches my life and I love him. There are a thousand ways he makes my life better, but mostly it's his cheerfulness I love the most.

EVALUATING THE AUTHOR'S ARGUMENTS:

Viewpoint author Amber M. Snyder describes adopting a dog that has mental health issues similar to her own. Should an animal with behaviors such as these be eligible to become an emotional support animal? Why or why not? What factors play into your opinion?

The Dangers of Fake Service Dogs

Brandy Arnold

"How can a restaurant know the difference between a real service dog and a fake service dog?"

In the following excerpted viewpoint, Brandy Arnold explores problems that arise when people fraudulently claim their animals as service animals. There is no official licensing for service animals, and anyone can buy vests, certification cards, and documents that look official. Thousands of people wrongly claim their animals as service animals. These animals are rarely properly trained and may even be dangerous in public. Their unruly behavior can bias businesses against true service animals. Brandy Arnold is a writer who has studied dog emotion and cognition through Duke University.

AS YOU READ, CONSIDER THE FOLLOWING QUESTIONS:
1. Do service dogs have to wear items that identify them?
2. What penalties does a business face if it asks people with service dogs to leave?
3. What is the danger in misrepresenting a pet as a service animal in public?

State and local governments, businesses, and nonprofit organizations that serve the public generally must allow service animals to accompany people with disabilities in all areas of the facility where the public is normally allowed to go. For example, in a hospital it would be inappropriate to exclude a service animal from areas such as patient rooms, clinics, cafeterias, or examination rooms. However, it may be appropriate to exclude a service animal from operating rooms or burn units where the animal's presence may compromise a sterile environment.

There are, however, some requirements. Service dogs must be leashed, harnessed, or tethered unless such a device would interfere with the dog's ability to perform his work, in which case the dog must be under full control of the handler through voice or hand signals.

Legitimate service dogs are well trained and a necessity to their handlers. They are trained to not be disruptive or cause a scene while in public. You will never see a service dog jumping up at people, barking or growling (unless alerting their handler to a problem), or even using the bathroom inappropriately.

Still, despite written laws the both define a service animal and explain the rights and requirements of service dog teams, the general public, including business owners and their staff, are largely unaware and misinformed.

Service dogs are NOT required to wear vests, collars, or bandanas that specifically identify them as a service animal, nor are the dogs or their handlers required to obtain certain licenses, identifications cards, or official certification. There is no central governing agency which either trains, certifies, or otherwise verifies the legitimacy of a service animal. There is no official training or obedience protocol that all service dogs must adhere to, simply that they cannot "cause a disturbance" while in public.

In fact, many legitimate, legal service dogs have been trained in the home setting, by their handler.

Although service dog vests, bandanas, or other forms of identification are not required, a vast majority of legitimate service dogs do wear them in a simple effort by their disabled handlers to avoid embarrassing, even disruptive or unsettling questions, to be left alone, or in hopes of peacefully going about their day without confrontation.

So, what's to prevent a person, like Forrest Brifton, from fraudulently strapping a service dog vest onto his dog, Chaco, and walking through his local mall?

Truthfully, not much.

While the federal government has done an excellent job of putting easily enforceable laws into place that provide and protect the rights of disabled persons and their service dogs at a national level, little has been done to prevent the fraudulent misrepresentation of family pets as service dogs.

Ambiguity in the definition of a service animal, lack of a central governing and certifying organization, and fear of both public backlash and costly litigation by business owners have created loopholes in the system that are big enough to drive a truck through—and people by the tens of thousands are taking advantage.

In fact, the laws are so vague that, prior to May 2011 when the ADA updated their definition of a service animal to only include dogs and, in some cases, miniature horses, it wasn't unheard of for people to claim a cat, a pet monkey, even an iguana was a legitimate service animal, thereby granting themselves the authority to bring those animals into restaurants, movie theaters, malls, banks, and precluding themselves from paying fees associated with bringing them into hotels, rental properties, and onboard airplanes—and, because businesses and staff don't understand the laws completely, they see a vest and ID card and believe the animal is legit!

A simple google search for "service dog vests" returns over 4 million hits from websites offering "official service dog" vests, certification cards, ID's, and official looking documents, some for the bargain basement price of $39. Many of these sites even provide customers with a written prescription, or "official" letter from a physician or psychiatrist detailing their "patient's" need for a service animal. Just answer a few yes or no questions in an online questionnaire and, voila!

It is estimated that there are roughly 20,000 true, legitimate service dog teams in the entire nation, yet hundreds of thousands of vests, certificates, and ID cards are sold every year. It is perfectly legal, in all 50 states, to buy, sell, and possess a service dog vest. The big business of selling such paraphernalia rakes in millions of dollars each year, from both those knowingly bucking the system and those who sincerely believe that answering a few questions and putting a vest and ID card on their dog makes them legit.

This pig is a member of the San Francisco International Airport's WAG Brigade, an initiative to ease airport passengers' travel anxieties.

Faking a service dog to gain access to public spaces is really not much different than using your grandmother's handicapped parking placard—with two major differences: it's easy to prove the placard isn't yours, and the penalties if you're caught are steep and easily enforceable.

Although the ADA's service dog policies apply on a national level, the enforcement of those policies falls under the responsibility of each state. To date, only 16 states have specific written laws pertaining either to the misrepresentation of a service dog or to misrepresenting oneself as disabled.

Despite all of the good established by ADA laws that protect the rights of the disabled, those same laws have left business owners and authorities with their hands tied. In an effort to protect the privacy of the disabled, very limited inquiries into the legitimacy of a service dog are allowed. Businesses, staff, and officials may legally only ask two questions to a service dog handler:

1. Is the dog a service animal required because of a disability?
2. What work or task has the dog been trained to perform?

It is unlawful to ask about a person's disability, require medical documentation, require a special identification card or training documentation for the dog, or ask that the dog demonstrate its ability to perform the work or task.

But, fixing the severely broken system isn't quite as easy as you might think.

Not only is it next to impossible to disprove the legitimacy of a service dog team, the risks of attempting to do so far outweigh the rewards. For example, if staff suspect that a person entering their place of business alongside a dog is fraudulently doing so, they can ask the above two questions—which a person passing their pet off as a service dog will have no moral issue lying about. Still not convinced, they may ask the person and their dog to leave.

It's very risky for businesses to deny access to people with service dogs, even when they suspect those dogs are merely pets. If they do so, and those suspicions prove to be unfounded, if the service dog team proves to be legitimate, they face serious civil penalties and fees upwards of $55,000 per offense.

Some people believe—regardless of the legislation—they have a right to take their dogs with them wherever they go. Places where dogs were traditionally not permitted are forced to look the other way because of the negative repercussions associated with denying entry to a service dog.

Last August, disabled veteran Richard Hunter was turned away from a Subway restaurant because of the presence of his service dog. A storm on social media followed.

How can a restaurant know the difference between a real service dog and a fake service dog? They can't. And that is the heart of the problem.

On the other hand, if a person is found to be faking a service dog—unless they're in one of those 16 states with written laws on the matter—they face no more than a proverbial slap on the wrist. Still, in those 16 states, the penalty is minor, usually a misdemeanor, and the fees typically range in the area of a few hundred dollars.

Unfortunately, we can't rely upon the moral fortitude of individuals or an honor system to prevent anyone with the inkling to do so from faking a service dog.

So, what makes fake service dogs such a real problem? It can be argued that the majority of people passing off their pets as service dogs aren't doing so with ill intent. Instead, they're simply trying to spend more time with the dogs they love. However, those people that fake service dogs don't consider the ripple effect of their actions.

True, legitimate service dogs are highly trained, incredibly well-mannered, and under the complete control of their handlers at all times whereas fake service dogs are often disruptive, they haven't had the hundreds of hours of training and socialization required to handle the tasks of a working dog. Likewise, their handlers often lack complete control over their dogs and don't appropriately handle having their access to public places challenged, as a trained service dog and an experienced handler with full knowledge of rights and responsibilities, as well as laws, would.

As a result, fake service dog teams create unnecessary discrimination toward legitimate teams. A business owner or their staff who has dealt with unruly behavior from a "faker" will immediately pass judgement on a true service dog team, the very minute they walk through the door. This discrimination leads to poor or even unlawful treatment of legitimate service dog teams in a variety of ways, like isolating them in an empty part of a restaurant, being ignored or overlooked by salespeople, following them around a store, etc.

Further, fake service dogs pose a genuine safety hazard not present in true service dogs. While service dogs are predictable, reliable, and trained to remain calm, quiet, and out of the way in a variety of circumstances, a family pet disguised as a service dog is most often not so reliable, making them a threat to both other patrons and to real service dogs that may enter the premises.

Disabled persons already inevitably deal with some form of bias or discrimination on a regular basis. The recent influx of fake service dog teams has created a culture where business owners and staff, more often than not, are suspicious of all service dog teams. Instead of assuming that most are legitimate and a rare few are fake, the common assumption is that most are fake and very few are real.

What can be done to solve the real problem of fake service dogs? The solution isn't entirely clear. While many have suggested the federal government take steps to create an official, legally recognized central registry, this solution could potentially infringe upon the privacy rights of the disabled.

In addition to a central registry, some argue that a specific, centralized training protocol needs to be established for all service dogs to adhere to. That program would include specific tasks that all registered service dogs must perform, like sitting under the table at a restaurant, not reacting to distractions, remaining calm at all times, staying out of the way, properly riding on an airplane, etc. However, since the tasks performed by service dogs vary so greatly from one handler to the next, developing a one-size-fits-all training program is an incredible—if not impossible—undertaking.

And then, there becomes the issue of providing resources for every single disabled person in the country to have access and the ability to become certified by a single, central agency, without creating excessive costs or infringing upon their rights.

There is no question, however, that those found to be misrepresenting their pet as a service dog need to be held accountable and legally reprimanded with stiff penalties that make the risk much greater than the reward. But without legislation, the problem will only escalate in the future.

In the meantime, more and more people are ordering service dog vests freely on the Internet.

EVALUATING THE AUTHOR'S ARGUMENTS:

In this viewpoint, the author argues that something should be done to prevent people from misrepresenting pets as service animals. Do you agree? Refer back to chapter 1, viewpoint 2, "There Are Rules for Businesses to Address Service Animals" for another view of the matter. Considering the challenges, what system do you think should be put in place, if any?

The System Needs an Overhaul

"ESAs are an epidemic, part of a zoo where entitlement, biting, pooping, and pretty much anything else goes."

Adrienne Matei

In the following viewpoint, Adrienne Matei notes that the number of people traveling with ESAs has exploded in recent years, leading to a wide range of problems. She acknowledges that while some of these people are selfish, others may genuinely feel their animals provide emotional support. One solution might be to integrate pets into more of our society. Another option would be to require stricter regulations on ESAs. Adrienne Matei is a writer and editor.

AS YOU READ, CONSIDER THE FOLLOWING QUESTIONS:
1. What motivates people to get ESA certifications for their pets?
2. Is an ESA intended to help anyone suffering from any kind of anxiety or mental illness?
3. How could "normalizing the presence of animals in more spaces" reduce the problem with false ESAs?

"The Number of Fake Emotional Support Dogs Is Exploding—Why?" by Adrienne Matei, Guardian News & Media Limited, August 13, 2019. Reprinted by permission.

According to her owner, Nick, 40, Rosie—a 50lb, eight-year-old yellow labrador retriever—is a very good girl. (Both man and dog are using a pseudonym for reasons which will be soon made clear.)

Much of Rosie's goodness is inherent, by virtue of her being a dog. But Rosie is not just a lovable creature, she is a helpful one, too. Rosie can open Nick's fridge for him. She can press handicap door activation buttons, heel off-leash on busy New York sidewalks, and she's even dabbled in a little search and rescue. She exhibits extreme self-control, especially when wearing her assistance animal vest, which she knows means she's on duty.

Nick doesn't fly with Rosie anymore, but when he did, she'd take up to 20 flights a year.

"When I went through the airport, people would come up to me and put their hand on my shoulder and say, 'It's so nice for you to travel with your dog,' or thank me for my service, thinking I was in the military," says Nick. "They clearly looked at Rosie, a lab, and just assumed I was in the military. I never lied, but that was the assumption people always made."

The assumption—that Nick is a veteran with an invisible disability like PTSD—is wrong. Nick has no disabilities, and Rosie is not his assistance animal. Instead, she's one of a growing number of pets whose owners have conscripted them into a life of duplicity.

To promote your pet to the status of an "emotional support animal," or ESA, all you need is a therapist's letter asserting the animal contributes to your psychological wellbeing. If you don't have a therapist, there are for-profit websites, known among some psychologists as "ESA mills," that will facilitate a quick, dubious disability appraisal by a clinician over the phone or via a web survey, then sell you miscellaneous swag like vests and tags (none of which are legally required for assistance animal owners to have) to make you pet look more official.

While ESAs are technically not legally allowed to venture everywhere in public with their owners (only service animals have that right), they do come with perks. Equipped with a therapist's letter, you may move your pet into an animal-free apartment or dormitory, and fly with your pet in a plane's cabin for free. And nothing stops ESA owners from asking for further accommodations.

Support Animal or Service Dog?

In 2014, the *New Yorker's* Patricia Marx gallivanted freely around the city with five successive fake ESA creatures, including a snake, an alpaca, and a pig named Daphne, demonstrating how easy it is to trick bewildered staff into letting random animals into their shops, museums, and restaurants.

While no governing body keeps track of the figure, a study from the University of California at Davis determined the number of ESAs registered by animal control facilities in the state increased 1,000% between 2002 and 2012. By 2015, the National Service Animal Registry, one of several sites that sell ESA certificates, had registered more than 65,000 assistance animals. In the four years since, that number increased 200%.

While not all spurious ESAs wreak havoc, some do—with serious consequences. In 2018, Delta Air reported an 84% surge in animal incidents since 2016, including urination, defecation and biting. Recent media reports of emotional support peacocks causing pandemonium in airports, comfort hamsters getting flushed in a frenzy, and dogs storming the stage during *Cats* have further contributed to the sense that ESAs are an epidemic, part of a zoo where entitlement, biting, pooping, and pretty much anything else goes.

For people who do have genuine disabilities, the situation is becoming untenable.

Ryan Honick, 33, whose service labrador, Pico, helps him with myriad daily tasks, says people on social media who broadcast their fraudulent pets infuriate him. Not only can fake ESAs distract or attack working service dogs, but service providers who have been inconvenienced by bad behavior from an unruly pet often sour on accommodating all animals thereafter. (Delta Air, for example, recently banned all ESAs from flights over eight hours.)

Despite having a federally protected service animal, Honick is often denied rides from rideshare drivers; he films these exchanges and keeps a running thread of them on his Twitter feed.

"I've had drivers ask me point blank, 'What happens when your dog defecates in my car?' I've said, 'That's not how trained service dogs function,'" says Honick. "People's perceptions get skewed because somebody brought in their misrepresented animal. And that makes

Caring for animals can be therapeutic. However, critics argue that the line between service animals and ESAs is being blurred.

it harder for people like me who have a legitimately trained dog like Pico, who's never caused any problems, because there's this wariness."

Honick advocates on behalf of Canine Companions for Independence, a not-for-profit group that assists people who require service animals to mitigate the effects of physical disabilities. He tries to educate others about the difference between service animals and ESAs, having found that the layperson often doesn't understand that a service dog is a $20,000 super-animal that can smell oncoming seizures or lead the blind, and currently an ESA is more like a pet who doesn't actively sabotage its owner's mental health.

Both have their merits, but only one is the difference between someone's life and death.

Under the Americans with Disabilities Act, only service animals like Pico have legal protections and the right to be with their owners in any space (airplanes and residential buildings have their own federal legislations recognizing both service animals and ESAs). Service animals can only be highly trained dogs or miniature horses capable of performing specific tasks. Emotional support animals can be any species or breed. They need no formal training, making them much more likely to spontaneously go a bit Jumanji.

It can be hard to know whether you're looking at a service dog or an ESA without asking the animal's owner, and even that can be tricky: you are legally only allowed to ask someone with a service animal two questions: "Is that a service animal?" and "What task is it trained to perform?"

Nothing can stop people from lying, or exploiting others' confusion by using the terms "service animal" and "ESA" interchangeably. "The majority of folks who slap a vest on their pet have already crossed that line," says Honick. "The easiest giveaway is behavior. A trained service animal is going to behave unobtrusively and professionally. If those things aren't happening, odds are high the animal is fraudulent."

For business owners wary of incurring a discrimination suit for kicking a llama out of their hotel bar, it often seems safer to just accommodate all assistance animals. Unchecked, fake and unfit ESAs continue to proliferate.

The Anxious Generation

At a glance, fake emotional support animals may look like a product of rampant entitlement, but they may reflect something more complex.

The National Institutes of Health reports that "studies have found that animals can reduce loneliness, increase feelings of social support, and boost your mood," and any pet owner can confirm that having an animal companion is one of the most effective non-pharmaceutical antidotes to anxiety you can get.

Meanwhile, generalized anxiety was identified relatively recently as a mental health condition and is only tentatively understood, but its reported levels are soaring across generations. The causes are frequently beyond our control, or feel like it (climate change, gun violence, financial stress), yet the responsibility to keep our mental health in check falls squarely on individuals. To feel passably well, we are told to exercise, get more sleep, eat wisely, and maybe snuggle a couple of corgis.

Perhaps that's why millennials, "the anxious generation," are also America's largest and most enthusiastic demographic of pet owners, with a 2018 survey reporting that of the 72% of millennials who own pets, 67% consider them their "fur babies"—or part of their families.

Surely, many people who get ESA certifications for their pets are selfishly motivated by convenience—they just want to bring their pets on to airplanes or into Starbucks. But others see it as a way to self-medicate without spending the time and money on an official psychological assessment to confirm what they already know: that anxiety is affecting their wellbeing.

Eliza (not her real name), 28, had no moral dilemma surrounding her decision to "register" her three-year-old pomsky, Buzz (also a pseudonym), through a website that also sold her an ESA tag, dog vest, and certificate.

"I haven't been diagnosed with any psychological illness, but I feel as if I naturally have a great deal of anxiety and I find that having my dog around me most of the time greatly reduces it," she says. "I see my pet as my family member; instead of a child I have a dog and I want to make sure he has the best quality of life."

Yet deriving comfort from pets doesn't entitle anyone to special treatment, especially when it comes at the expense of disabled persons. And while anxiety is a difficult condition, its intensity falls on a spectrum; official ESAs are intended to aid those who suffer only from its most debilitating manifestations.

Despite Rosie's good behavior, Nick's conscience eventually caught up with him, and he ceased flying with her masquerading as his assistance animal in 2017.

"When I started flying with Rosie, it wasn't quite the thing that it is now," he says, noting he came to feel that too many people were trying to "get behind the system" with untrained dogs. "Sometimes you could tell the dogs were uncomfortable traveling, that they were scared, they were distracting real service animals, and at that point I didn't want to be part of it any more."

"Not Just Any Pet"

The question is, short of relying on everyone's moral compass kicking in, how do we cut down on fraudulent ESAs?

One solution could be a collective movement towards an increasingly pet-integrated society. A small number of colleges permit pets in dormitories, a policy more could consider. Normalizing the presence of animals in more spaces may reduce the impetus for people to game the mental health system just to spend more time with their dogs.

But the more likely and impactful fix might be a change in medical policy.

According to Cassie Boness, University of Missouri PhD candidate and co-author of an article on tightening ESA regulations published by the American Psychological Association this month, the professionals who sign off on ESA letters need to adhere to a strict and standardized evaluation model.

Her research proposes a four-point evaluation system developed to empirically ensure not only that the individual in question suffers from a psychological disability that impairs their functioning, but that the specific animal they want to certify both behaves appropriately to access the spaces where they are permitted and objectively improves their handler's symptoms.

Boness and her colleagues hope their new regulations will be adopted and formalized by the American Psychological Association, but they expect backlash from scammers of all stripes.

In fact, guidelines would help anyone who requires an assistance animal: "As we have more clear guidelines, ESAs will hopefully start to be more well respected, because not just any pet can be certified," says Boness. With stronger regulations in place, the dog days of dubious ESA certifications will be over. Until then, we're left with a failing honor system rife with confusion, selfishness, and profiteers.

EVALUATING THE AUTHOR'S ARGUMENTS:

Viewpoint author Adrienne Matei offers possible responses to false emotional support animals. One would be to make pets more acceptable in various areas of life. Another would be to require stricter regulations on ESAs. Do you support either of these answers? Why or why not? What problems could result from each?

Think of the Anxious Animals

Christine Calder

"In recent years, the number of animals flying in the cabin on airplanes has increased exponentially."

In the following viewpoint, Christine Calder shares concerns about animals on planes. Government agencies considered requiring a veterinarian to certify that an ESA would behave onboard, something that veterinarians cannot vouch for. Subsequently, vets might refuse to fill out the required forms, and true service animals could be denied air transportation. The author also notes that many animals are stressed by air travel, which can lead to problem behavior. Christine Calder is a veterinarian who specializes in animal behavior.

AS YOU READ, CONSIDER THE FOLLOWING QUESTIONS:
1. Do people flying with an ESA pay more or less than someone traveling with an animal merely identified as a pet?
2. How can ESAs trigger stress in other people?
3. How do some animals suffer from traveling on planes?

"Flying with Emotional Support Animals: The Ups and Downs of Life in Coach," Christine Calder, The Conversation, November 19, 2018. https://theconversation.com/flying-with-emotional-support-animals-the-ups-and-downs-of-life-in-coach-102022. Licensed under CC BY-ND 4.0.

The Department of Transportation has been considering new guidelines for flying with emotional support animals since spring 2018, but it doesn't look like those guidelines will be ready in time for the holiday travel season.

No one knows whether the new guidelines could have helped recent Delta Air Lines passenger Matthew Meehan, who claimed that he had to sit in doggie poop from an emotional support animal on a Nov. 1, 2018 flight from Atlanta to Miami. The dog became sick on a previous flight, the airline reported, leaving the mess for Meehan.

And that was after Delta tightened its rules for flying with emotional support animals.

In recent years, the number of animals flying in the cabin on airplanes has increased exponentially, due to an increase of these emotional support animals. United Airlines reported a 77 percent rise in just one year of emotional support animals. These animals fly for free, and sometimes they and their human are upgraded to first class to avoid a kerfuffle in coach.

As an assistant clinical professor of veterinary medicine and veterinary behaviorist, I have experience in small animal care and animal behavior, and I am concerned about the welfare of animals on planes as well as the humans. The issues are more complicated than many imagine.

Stressed Out by Flying? Aren't We All.

Emotional support animals differ from trained service animals, who have been trained to do work or perform a task for the benefit of a person with a disability. Most emotional support animals are not officially trained to offer support, but their owners consider them a comfort nonetheless.

Some people who need trained service animals have grown weary of emotional support animals. Many resent their work animals being lumped in with emotional support animals, whom they consider poseurs. Many also claim that their service animals are being turned away from flights in the wake of tighter restrictions imposed by some airlines.

Oscar Munoz, CEO of United Airlines, told a business group that the situation aboard has become so ludicrous that his airline was expected to fly a support animal for an emotional support animal.

Last year, United drew a line in the sky when a passenger wanted to fly with an emotional support peacock.

For American Airlines, the last straw was a goat (miniature horses are still allowed). American issued new guidelines in July that also restrict support animals from occupying a seat or nibbling food from a tray table. There's no mention about whether they can drink on board. Pet owners, however, claim that it is discriminatory to deny them the comfort of emotional support animals.

The DOT and other government agencies have been exploring a revision in the laws. These stricter proposals have received revision requests and support from both the American Veterinary Medical Association and the Association of Flight Attendants-CWA Union.

The American Veterinary Medical Association pushed back on language, however, that would have made its members accountable for verifying that an animal will behave, because there is no way to guarantee the behavior of an animal.

A Long History

This all took off when the 1986 federal Air Carrier Access Act allowed people with mental health disabilities to fly on a plane with an animal free of charge, if it alleviates the person's condition.

Over the years, however, airlines have said that some animal-carrying passengers abuse the rules so they can simply fly with their pets for free. Some want to prevent their pets from flying in cargo, where some pets have died.

Many passengers traveling without animals have said they are stressed by emotional support animals. Animals trigger phobias in some people and allergies in others; about 10 percent of the human population is allergic to animals. Cats bear most of the blame, but proteins in dog dander and even saliva can cause an allergic reaction.

FAST FACT

Animals can suffer from stress when in enclosed spaces, among crowds of people, or exposed to loud noises. A stressed animal might growl, snap, or bite.

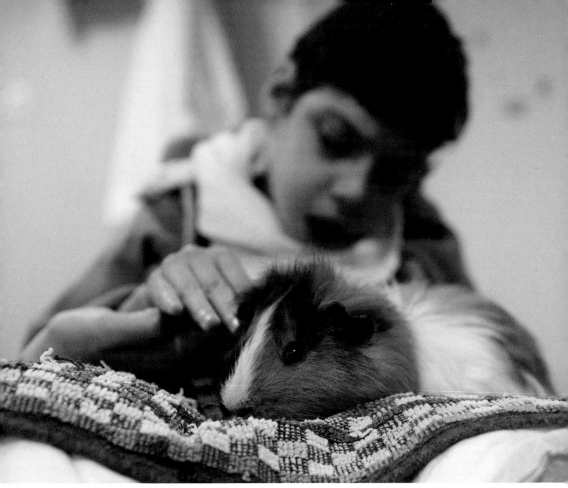

Even guinea pigs can take part in animal-assisted therapy.

Many airlines now require advance notification. Many also want a diagnosis letter for the human stating that the person is psychologically disabled and can not be without the stability provided by that pet. Writing such a letter can pose risks and ethical dilemmas for psychologists, however, a study suggested. Nonetheless, people seeking a letter can usually obtain one online.

The airline industry also considered asking for documentation from a veterinarian that the animal can behave in public and that it is healthy and has been vaccinated. The American Veterinary Medical Association emphasized to the DOT that veterinarians cannot vouch for animals' behavior and that expanding the scope of the veterinary form could lead to refusals by veterinarians to fill out these forms.

That, in turn, could result in certified service animals being denied air transportation.

The airlines dropped that requirement. Instead, many airlines ask that the animal just be clean and not have an odor.

Who's Right?

There's a lot of scientific evidence that being in close proximity to, and living with, companion animals has many psychological and physiological benefits for humans. In children, animal-assisted therapy has been shown to reduce pain perception and provide better coping skills in the hospital environment. Another study found that in children with autism, social behaviors increased in the presence of animals compared to toys.

Studies also have shown a positive effect of service dogs on war veterans and people with traumatic brain injuries.

But do emotional support animals really help people more than traditional pets?

According to a 2016 literature review by two psychologists and a psychology graduate student, the answer is no. There is little evidence to support that emotional support animals are more effective than traditional pets.

In fact, there are no specific guidelines or standards for evaluating emotional support animals. And, without standards, legal protection is complicated when incidents occur, such as when a pit bull bites a person, as one did on a Delta Air Lines flight, leading the airline to ban that breed.

Is It Good for the Goose Just Because It's Good for the Human?

There's also evidence that the animals themselves may not fare so well. Riding on planes, being in closed-in spaces, and being exposed to loud noises and crowds of people can be overstimulating and scary to an animal, especially one not accustomed to that particular environment.

In a 2002 study, researchers looked at air travel in beagles. They found that blood and salivary cortisol was much higher than baseline in dogs during air transport, an indication they were stressed. The authors noted that just because the beagles were mainly inactive during transport did not mean they were not stressed. Rather, their behavior indicated that the beagles adopted a conservative-withdrawal approach in response to their stress, rather than fight-or-flight.

In contrast, service dogs are often genetically selected and extensively trained for the tasks they will perform. They need consistent and predictable behaviors in a wide range of situations and environments in order to safely provide service to their humans, especially if a life depends on that particular service.

Training, training methods, the trainer and training tools used can also have a significant effect on behavior and coping skills in animals.

And, whenever an animal is fearful or anxious, he may be more likely to choose an aggression strategy, such as growling, snapping or biting, especially if he feels cornered or trapped. In the end, airlines and regulators are left to develop ways to avoid the downsides of comfort animals, even as consumers have come to expect this accommodation.

EVALUATING THE AUTHOR'S ARGUMENTS:

Viewpoint author Christine Calder notes that air travel can be stressful for animals. Consider this in addition to the arguments made in the previous two viewpoints. Does the new information presented here change your views at all? If so, how?

Facts About Service, Emotional Support, and Therapy Animals

Editor's note: These facts can be used in reports to add credibility when making important points or claims.

Assistance animals can be divided into three general categories: service animals, therapy animals, and emotional support animals.

Service animals include dogs and miniature horses. They are trained to perform tasks that ease their handlers' disabilities. They may help people who are visually impaired or hearing impaired, who use wheelchairs, or who have a variety of other special needs. In the US, an estimated 500,000 service dogs assist people.

The International Association of Assistance Dog Partners (IAADP) sets minimum training standards for public access. They recommend 120 hours of schooling over a period of six months or more. At least 30 hours should be devoted to outings. The dog should also be trained in obedience tasks and tasks related to the specific disability.

Therapy dogs provide therapy to people other than their handlers. Therapy animals may help people make physical or mental improvements. Animals can also provide emotional support to people who are sad, lonely, or bored. Most of the evidence for the benefit of therapy animals is anecdotal.

A number of animal assisted therapy programs exist. Some encourage children to read to dogs. Others help people with physical therapy. At disaster sites, animals may help people process emotions.

Therapy dogs are not trained service dogs. However, they and their owners are trained to interact with people safely. Unlike service dogs, therapy dogs interact with a variety of people. They may visit schools, day cares, nursing homes, hospitals, etc. They must have friendly, easy-going personalities. While there are not yet standards of training, typically therapy animals require weeks of training with their handlers.

An emotional support animal (ESA) is a pet that alleviates symptoms of an emotional or mental disability through companionship and affection. The effectiveness of emotional support animals has not been studied in depth.

By law, an ESA must be prescribed to a patient by a licensed mental health professional, like a therapist, psychologist, or psychiatrist. People request emotional support animals for many conditions, including anxiety, depression, post-traumatic stress disorder, bipolar disorder, social anxiety, and phobias. Getting a letter identifying a pet as an ESA is fairly easy. Scam companies offer ESA letters without a doctor's referral.

Rights of Assistance Animals

Assistance animals provide the owner with certain rights. These rights are different depending on whether an animal is a service animal or an emotional support animal. ESAs do not have the same rights as service dogs, such as access to restaurants. However, they do have some rights, such as the ability to live in housing that does not normally accept pets. The rules for service animals are covered under the Americans with Disabilities Act (ADA).

Business owners and staff are only allowed to ask two questions of anyone bringing in an animal they say is a service animal:
1. Is your animal required because of a disability?
2. What work or task is it trained to perform?

They cannot demand documentation. They cannot ask about someone's disability or ask the animal to demonstrate the task.

Service animals are not required to wear vests or other items that identify them as service animals, but many service animals do use identifying clothing. This lets people know the animal is working and helps the handler avoid questions and harassment.

There is no official licensing for service animals, and anyone can buy vests, certification cards, and documents that look official. Most states do not have laws that would punish people for misrepresenting themselves or their animals. Thousands of people wrongly claim their animals as service animals. These animals are rarely properly trained and may even be dangerous in public. Their unruly behavior can bias businesses against true service animals.

Disability in America

According to the ADA, an individual with a disability is a person who has a physical or mental impairment that substantially limits one or more major life activities, has a record of such an impairment, or is regarded as having such an impairment. The ADA does not name all of the impairments that are covered.

Over 50 million American adults have disabilities. It is estimated that 10 percent of people in the US have a medical condition that could be considered an invisible disability. Invisible or hidden disabilities are those that are not immediately apparent. They include chronic pain, chronic fatigue, mental illness, chronic dizziness, sleep disorders, and diabetes if those conditions impair normal activities. Vision and hearing problems may also be invisible.

Organizations to Contact

The editors have compiled the following list of organizations concerned with the issues debated in this book. The descriptions are derived from materials provided by the organizations. All have publications or information available for interested readers. The list was compiled on the date of publication of the present volume; the information provided here may change. Be aware that many organizations take several weeks or longer to respond to inquiries, so allow as much time as possible for the receipt of requested materials.

Animal Assisted Intervention International (AAII)
contact form: aai-int.org/contact-us/
website: www.aai-int.org/
This organization supports people working in the field of animal assisted therapy, education, and activities.

Assistance Dogs International, Inc. (ADI)
contact form: assistancedogsinternational.org/forms/contact-us/
website: www.assistancedogsinternational.org/
ADI is a worldwide coalition of not-for-profit programs that train and place assistance dogs. Website resources include information about public access laws and travel resources.

Can Do Canines
9440 Science Center Drive
New Hope, MN 55428
(763) 331-3000
contact form: can-do-canines.org/contact/
website: www.can-do-canines.org/
This organization is "dedicated to enhancing the quality of life for people with disabilities by creating mutually beneficial partnerships with specially trained dogs." Learn about their dogs and how they are

trained, and see volunteer opportunities such as fostering a dog or dog walking.

Canine Companions for Independence
PO Box 446
Santa Rosa, CA 95402-0446
(800) 572-2275
contact: visit the website for contact options
website: www.cci.org/
Canine Companions for Independence provides assistance dogs free of charge to recipients. On the website, donate, order a puppy calendar, check out the latest news, or get tips on disabilities and assistance dogs.

Guide Horse Foundation
PO Box 511
Kittrell, NC 27544
(252) 431-0050
email: info@guidehorse.com
website: www.guide-horse.org/
This foundation explores options for providing miniature horses as guide animals for visually impaired people. Learn how and why miniature horses make good guide animals.

Helping Hands: Monkey Helpers for the Disabled
541 Cambridge Street
Boston, MA 02134
(617) 787-4419
email: info@monkeyhelpers.org
website: www.monkeyhelpers.org/
Since 1979, this group has been helping adults with mobility impairments live more independent lives by providing trained service monkeys to help with daily tasks.

The International Association of Assistance Dog Partners (IAADP)
PO Box 638
Sterling Heights, MI 48311

(888) 544-2237
email: mc.iaadp@gmail.com
website: www.iaadp.org
This nonprofit organization represents people partnered with guide, hearing, and service dogs. The website offers information and resources on assistance dogs and advocacy efforts.

NEADS World Class Service Dogs
PO Box 1100
Princeton, MA 01541
(978) 422-9064
contact page: neads.org/contact
website: https://neads.org/
This nonprofit organization has trained over 1,800 service dogs. Learn about its programs, how dogs and clients are trained, and ways to get involved.

Paws with a Cause
4646 S. Division
Wayland, MI 49348
(616) 877-7297
email: paws@pawswithacause.org
website: www.pawswithacause.org/
This group aims to enhance the independence and quality of life for people with disabilities through trained assistance dogs, as well as to increase awareness of the rights and roles of assistance dogs.

Pet Partners
345 118th Avenue SE, Suite 200
Bellevue, WA 98005
(425) 679-5500
contact form: petpartners.org/about-us/contact-us/
website: www.petpartners.org/
This charity's mission is "to improve human health and well-being through the human-animal bond." The website has webinars, a blog, and other information. Learn about reading to pets or becoming a volunteer therapy team with your animal.

For Further Reading

Books

Brooks, Megan. *Training Your Own Service Dog* (The Complete Guide Series: How to Train Service Dogs). Gainesville, FL: MegaBooks, 2020. This book provides comprehensive information on owner-training an assistance dog. The book covers the laws on service dogs, ESAs, and therapy dogs.

Cabri Media. *Assistance Animal Laws: Learn Your Rights Regarding Service Animals, Emotional Support Animals, Therapy Pets, and Other Dogs, Cats & Assistance Animals*. Cabri Media, 2017. The author explains the rights and obligations surrounding service and emotional support animals, in housing, on the job, traveling, and in businesses.

Fine, Aubrey H. *Handbook on Animal-Assisted Therapy: Foundations and Guidelines for Animal-Assisted Interventions*. Cambridge, MA: Academic Press, 2019. This title highlights advances in the field of animal assisted therapy. It is directed at therapists considering incorporating animal assisted therapy into their practices.

Grace, Keagen J. *The Ultimate Service Dog Training Manual: 100 Tips for Choosing, Raising, Socializing, and Retiring Your Dog*. New York, NY: Skyhorse, 2020. A dog trainer covers "everything you need to know about obtaining, training, and living with service dogs."

Hack, Jennifer. *Service Dog Training Guide: A Step-by-Step Training Program for You and Your Dog*. Emeryville, CA: Rockridge Press, 2020. Step-by-step instructions explain how to teach a dog everything from retrieving items to reminding someone to take medication.

Matthews, Max. *Training Your Own Psychiatric Service Dog: Step by Step Guide to Training Your Own Psychiatric Service Dog*. Independently published, 2018. This book covers everything from how to select a suitable service dog to what is expected in public access areas.

Sanchez, Veronica. *Service Dog Coaching: A Guide for Pet Dog Trainers*. Wenatchee, WA: Dogwise Publishing, 2019. This author teaches professional trainers how to help owners with disabilities train a service dog.

Taylor, Stephanie L. *Animals That Heal: The Role of Service Dogs and Emotional Support Animals in Mental Health Treatment*. Independently published, 2018. This handbook was written by a service dog handler. She explains "everything you need to know about animals that heal."

Tedeschi, Philip. *Transforming Trauma: Resilience and Healing Through Our Connections with Animals* (New Directions in the Human-Animal Bond). West Lafayette, IN: Purdue University Press, 2019. International experts cover a wide range of topics relating to animals' ability to help humans, especially in regards to coping with trauma.

Periodicals and Internet Sources

Allison, Rory, "Complete List of Pros and Cons of Having a Service Dog or Service Animal," September 1, 2018. https://www .theservicedogs.com/complete-list-of-pros-and-cons-of-having-a -service-dog-or-service-animal/

Alt, Kimberly, "Service Dog vs Therapy Dog vs Emotional Support Dogs," Canine Journal, July 10, 2017. https://www.caninejournal .com/service-dog-vs-therapy-dog-vs-emotional-support-dogs/

AVMA Public Policy/Animal Welfare Division, "Assistance Animals: Rights of Access and the Problem of Fraud," April 21, 2017. https:// www.avma.org/sites/default/files/resources/Assistance -Animals-Rights-Access-Fraud-AVMA.pdf

Barth, F. Diane, "Is an Emotional Support Animal Serving a Person's Needs or Their Narcissism?" NBC News, June 29, 2019. https:// www.nbcnews.com/think/opinion/emotional-support-animal -serving-person-s-needs-or-their-narcissism-ncna1024586

Brueck, Hilary, "United Just Banned 'Emotional Support Animals' on Long Flights—and Science Is on the Airline's Side," *Business Insider*, January 7, 2019. https://www.businessinsider.com/emotional -support-animals-science-psychology-2018-3

Herzog, Hal, PhD, "Emotional Support Animals: The Therapist's Dilemma," *Psychology Today*, July 19, 2016. https://www .psychologytoday.com/us/blog/animals-and-us/201607 /emotional-support-animals-the-therapists-dilemma

Iannuzzi, Dorothea, and Andrew N. Rowan, "Ethical Issues in Animal -Assisted Therapy Programs," Anthrozoös, April 27, 2015. https:// doi.org/10.2752/089279391787057116

Marino, Lori, "Construct Validity of Animal-Assisted Therapy and Activities: How Important Is the Animal in AAT?" Anthrozoös, April 28, 2015. https://doi.org/10.2752/175303712X13353430377219

Marino, Lori, "Do Emotional Support Animals Need Emotional Support?" *Psychology Today*, September 16, 2019. https://www .psychologytoday.com/us/blog/animals-and-us/201909/do -emotional-support-animals-need-emotional-support

Mishi, "Emotional Support Dog – Pros and Cons of the ESA Trend." https://mishipets.com/emotional-support-dog/

Moosh, "Are There Any Financial Aid Programs for Emotional Support Animals?" https://mooshme.com/financial-aid-programs -emotional-support-animals/

Moosh, "How Pet Food Banks Help ESA Owners on Low Incomes." https://mooshme.com/pet-food-banks-help-esa-owners-low-incomes/

Moosh, "Pros and Cons of an Emotional Support Animal in California." https://mooshme.com/pros-cons-emotional-support -animal-california/

ProCare Therapy, "The Pros and Cons of Therapy Dogs," October 1, 2019. http://blog.procaretherapy.com/working-in-schools/the -pros-and-cons-of-therapy-dogs/

Resnick, Brian, "The Surprisingly Weak Scientific Case for Emotional Support Animals," Vox, November 19, 2018. https://www.vox.com /science-and-health/2018/2/23/17012116/emotional-support -animal-airplane-psychology-research-dogs

Rucker, Margie, "The Truth About Service Dogs," AKC Reprinted from *The Canine Chronicle*, March 18, 2015. https://www.akc.org /expert-advice/news/the-truth-about-service-dogs/

Stockman, Farah, "People Are Taking Emotional Support Animals Everywhere. States Are Cracking Down," *New York Times*, June 18, 2019. https://www.nytimes.com/2019/06/18/us/emotional -support-animal.html

Weber, Kylee, "Emotional Support Animals: Making the Best Decision," The Campus, October 5, 2019. http://www.oucampus.org/news/view.php/1039183/Emotional-support-animals-making-the-bes

Weiner, Lena J., "3 Misconceptions About Emotional Support Animals," Health Leaders, January 11, 2016. https://www.healthleadersmedia.com/strategy/3-misconceptions-about-emotional-support-animals

Witz, Billy, "Emotional Support, with Fur, Draws Complaints on Planes," *New York Times*, November 15, 2013. https://www.nytimes.com/2013/11/16/business/emotional-support-with-fur-draws-complaints-on-planes.html

Websites

Affordable Service Dog Training by Top Dogs (www.topdogservicedogs.org)
This nonprofit organization based in Tucson, Arizona, teaches people with disabilities how to train their own dogs as certified service dogs. See past newsletters on the website.

American Veterinary Medical Association (www.avma.org)
AVMA is an organization for veterinarians. Resources include information on animal health and welfare, including a 15-page report on "Assistance Animals: Rights of Access and the Problem of Fraud."

Great Plains Assistance Dogs Foundation (www.greatplainsdogs.com/)
Get tips for training a dog, from housebreaking a new puppy to teaching fun tricks.

National Service Animal Registry (www.nsarco.com)
NSAR is a service dog registry "committed to helping the disabled enjoy the benefits of a service dog or ESA." The site discusses different types of support animals, how to get your animal to qualify, and rights for people with support animals.

Index

and differences from service
animals, 17–18, 42,
45–52, 68, 69, 101
ESA letters/certification, 8,
31, 41–44, 49, 54–55,
56, 57, 59
traveling with, 8, 42, 49–50,
53–61, 93–99, 100–105
epilepsy, 69, 72
Eustis, Dorothy Harrison, 12
EZCare Medical Clinic, 41–44

F
Fair Housing Act, 50, 51
fake service animals,
dangers of, 9, 52, 86–92,
93–99
Falteisek, Laura, 59
Frank, Morris, 12

G
George-Michalson, Nancy, 26
German shepherds, as guide
dogs, 12
Good Dog Foundation, 27, 28
Great Plains Assistance Dogs
Foundation, 14
Grové, Christine, 35–39
guide dogs for the visually
impaired, history of, 12

H
hearing dogs, 13–14
Henderson, Linda, 35–39

Honick, Ryan, 95–96
Hunter, Richard, 90

I
International Association of
Assistance Dog Partners,
70, 71, 72
invisible/hidden disabilities, 64,
67, 68, 69, 77, 94, 108

J
Jackson, Marlin, 58

L
Labrador-golden retriever
crosses, as guide dogs, 12
Labrador retrievers, as guide
dogs, 12
Leduc, Marie Eve, 65–66
licensing/certification of assistance animals, 9, 20, 87

M
Marx, Patricia, 95
Massachusetts Society for the
Prevention of Cruelty to
Animals–Angell, 45–52
Massey, J. Ross, 58
Matei, Adrienne, 93–99
McElroy, Bridgette, 26
McPherson, Rachel, 27–28, 29
Meehan, Matthew, 101
Meltzer, Marisa, 53–61

traveling with emotional support animals, 8, 42, 49–50, 53–61, 93–99, 100–105
Truitt, Taylor, 56
Tutin, Judith, 30–34

U

United Airlines, 57, 101, 102
US Department of Transportation, 50, 57, 71, 101, 102, 103

V

Ventiko, 57–58

Picture Credits